F.E.E.L.

FEEL EVERY EMOTION AS LOVE

LIVING SOURCE PUBLISHING

F.E.E.L.: Feel Every Emotion as Love
© 2012 by Michelle Bersell

Living Source Publishing

ISBN: 978-0-9801413-1-3
Library of Congress Control Number: 2012915484
Printed in the United States of America

F.E.E.L.

FEEL EVERY EMOTION AS LOVE

Turn Your Negative Feelings into Your Greatest Allies

Michelle Bersell, M.A., M.Ed.

LIVING SOURCE PUBLISHING

CONTENTS

PART I

EMOTIONAL AWARENESS

PART II

MINEFIELDS: UNDERSTANDING AND
LOVING YOUR EGO AND FEARS

PART III

FEEL EVERY EMOTION AS LOVE

DEDICATED

To my loving husband, for believing
To my amazing kids, for inspiring
To my supportive parents, for caring
And to those of you who have the courage to feel deeply,
for you are my soul family.

God turns you from one feeling to another
and teaches by means of opposites,
so that you will have two wings to fly with, not one.

—RUMI

INTRODUCTION

AS YOU GO THROUGH THE DAY, DO NEGATIVE FEELINGS SOME-times get in the way of living the good life? They can certainly drain the energy right out of you and take you down a painful path for seemingly no good reason at all...except, it appears, to periodically torture you.

I know what it's like to want to get rid of negative feelings. Having bouts of negative feelings roll in and out of your life takes your energy away from the fully expressed, joyful, balanced you.

Within your heart, you carry a knowingness that you are meant to share more of yourself in the world. You may not be completely clear what your unique expression is exactly, or how you want to express it. Your heart only knows that this fully ex-pressed version of you longs to *shine* from the inside-out. You even have moments when you are deeply connected to living this way. You feel yourself shining from within and sense the exhilaration. You feel inspired, motivated, and in the flow of life.

Suddenly, the responsibilities of the day start to pull at you. An important email, phone call, document, or person needs your attention. A baby starts crying or your kid comes home from school upset. You feel a sense of pressure to keep forging ahead toward the daily obligations that await you.

You also have days when, if you were to take a step back, you would marvel at how well you handled your day. (Perhaps you already do!) Other days, your feelings start to get to you, and suddenly you find yourself feeling overwhelmed, exhausted, or confused. You may become frustrated, sad, angry, anxious, or filled with guilt, and your gusto for life is temporarily down the drain.

Whoa! What happened? What went wrong?

You can't quite figure it out. All you know is that you want those negative feelings to go away so you can get your mojo back. You pull out your personal development toolkit and use some tried-and-true methods to turn your feelings around and get back to a more uplifted state. You engage in positive thinking, you journal, or you apply other techniques to free yourself energetically from the negative feelings.

Success! Your methods worked...in the short term. But the next day or week, or perhaps even later in the month (you know, ladies, during that special time when Auntie Flo pays a visit), the negative feelings are back. Your mojo is missing again, and you've got to whip out those tools and techniques, yet again, to release the unwanted feelings that deflate you.

I used to live this way once too. As a psychotherapist and life coach, I had oodles of tools and techniques to help me whisk away my negative feelings—methods that had served me very well in escaping the confines of a boxed-in life. Those tools and techniques would release me from my negative feelings just long enough for me to reach up and lift the lid of the box.

With the box open, I learned to become more comfortable in my own skin. Feeling more comfortable allowed me to be more open to the yearnings of my heart. Those yearnings were telling me that there was more of myself that I wanted to share. I wanted to live bolder. I wanted to *shine!*

The problem was that my heart's version of life wasn't quite happening. Sure, I would make a few strides forward. Yet time and again, I would find my negative feelings creeping back in with self-doubt, confusion, or even paralysis.

I began to ask myself whether there was something inherently wrong with me. I wondered if I was one of those who didn't get the so-called "happy gene." After all, I had degrees in clinical psychology and life coaching. Why couldn't I just feel happy and self-confident so I could stay on course?

Besides becoming annoyed and frustrated by my negative feelings, I felt like I surely must be doing something wrong to feel the way I did. Everything I had studied and learned seemed to underscore how my negative feelings were the culprits. If I could just learn to get rid of them once and for all, I thought, I would be good to go. The problem was, even with all the training and studying I had done, nothing was working on me to completely banish those feelings.

I just didn't get it. I found myself asking, *What the heck is the purpose of negative feelings, anyway? Why are they here? More important, why don't they just leave me alone?*

After years of dedicating my life to my passion of understanding emotional well-being, I felt that something was amiss. What was I missing? What else did I need to know? Why did we have negative feelings at all?

THE CALLING

As it turned out, my questions regarding emotional well-being would soon be answered from within. For nine months straight, I was awakened at 4:30 each morning with a directive from a little voice inside my head telling me, *"Get up and write!"*

What I learned from that nine-month period had never been taught to me in all my years of study in a clinical psychology program, in the numerous spiritual books I had read, or through the training in holistic modalities I had received as I became a life coach. What I learned was completely new and was about to turn upside down the way I understood feelings.

As words flowed through me in those wee hours of the morning, what I learned was that the way we currently understand our feelings, and in particular our negative feelings, is one-sided. As we use the tools and techniques available today for dealing with negative feelings, the whole point is to get rid of, free ourselves from, or sidestep these uncomfortable emotions. Experiencing negative feelings is viewed as a problem, plain and simple. From this perspective, our job is to dispense with our negative feelings, as much as possible, in order to feel freer, more alive, and joy-filled.

What if the opposite were true? Rather than trying to distance ourselves energetically from our negative feelings because we felt that they got in the way of our happiness, what if we saw them as enhancing our lives? Could there actually be a different meaning to our negative feelings than the one we currently assign to them?

YES, THERE IS!

LEAVING THE EMOTIONAL STONE AGE BEHIND

Up until now, when you've experienced a negative emotion, it's likely been accompanied by negative internal messages about life and about yourself and others. I too had that experience whenever negative feelings arose. In fact, negative messages about myself seemed to become more deeply ingrained by my negative feelings. No wonder we all want to distance ourselves from negative emotions when their calling card is battered self-images and general negativity!

What if there were another side to our negative feelings that we haven't been privy to until now? What if we were to flip the coin over, so to speak, and discover the same negative feelings, only now attached to completely different messages? These messages might offer insight, specific guidance, and clarity to help us identify the wisest course of action. Such messages would be filled with love, empowering us to live more fully expressed lives —to *shine*!

Let me be clear that we are not talking about simply slapping a positive slant onto a negative feeling. We all know that that doesn't work. Doing so only makes the negative feeling pop right back up a few moments, hours, or days later. We're too smart to con ourselves like that. Our inner wisdom won't allow us to get away with just trying to put a positive spin on something which, at our core, needs our attention.

Here's the exciting news: *Your negative feelings are trying to get your attention!* They're not doing this just to beat you up with self-loathing talk, as your short-sighted ego has conditioned you to believe. Your negative feelings come up to signal to you when you are going off course *because you are unconsciously being run by your fears.*

Think about it. If you are not conscious of your fears, how are you going to recognize that you are off the mark? You need some type of alert to get you back on track with your heart's desires; otherwise, your ego is just going to keep tripping you up.

As I explored my own emotional responses, I was astounded

to find that each specific negative emotion offered unique guidance. In other words, there is a reason why we might feel sadness in a given moment, for example, rather than anxiety. Whichever particular emotion is triggered, it is there because we need the guidance of that specific feeling in that particular situation to get us back on course.

Isn't this amazing? It was for me, because it meant that instead of continuing to try to ignore my negative feelings (something I sucked at anyway), I finally understood that my negative feelings were on my side. Rather than continue to try to get rid of them, I could actually learn how to use them to serve me. My negative feelings now became my greatest allies!

My deepest desire is that your negative feelings become your greatest allies as well, because, let me tell you, life feels so much freer this way. What happens is this: When you learn how to take the fear out of your negative feelings, they actually provide support as you transform your life. Bit by bit, emotion by emotion, they identify and help you to address those areas that are unconscious energy leaks. These same negative feelings also come with the built-in energy to propel you out of your comfort zone and illuminate your path. This means you are constantly being referred to auto-correct, when veering off your path, and then supported in your actions, even when they are outside of your comfort zone.

Here is why shifting out of the emotional Stone Age changes everything:

In the emotional Stone Age, negative feelings are seen as menacing stones on your path, eager to get in your way and trip you up. Rather than continue to look at negative feelings as stumbling stones to be kicked aside or navigated around, the shift is about learning to see them as bearing insightful messages direct from your inner wisdom. Instead of carrying a heavy millstone or expending energy trying to throw off the stone, you learn how to navigate with greater ease and agility *because of the stone.*

I call this very major shift in perception *F.E.E.L. (Feel Every Emotion as Love)* because love, from my perspective, is the opposite of fear, the place from which negative feelings are currently understood. By learning how to F.E.E.L., rather than simply feel, you are able to read your negative feelings from the higher vibration of love rather than fear. Through the lens of love, you clearly recognize why each particular emotion has shown up on your path, and the important information it has for you!

Through F.E.E.L., you train yourself to hear your empowered self rather than the voice of your fear. When your empowered self comes through, you receive:

- Clarity regarding your true path,
- Guidance as to the exact next step to take,
- Inspiration and loving messages, encouraging you to take action on behalf of your highest good, and
- Energy and motivation to break out of your comfort zone.

Emotions are the fuel for your intentions. You need your emotional energy to fire you up and make your heart's desires a reality. In the emotional Stone Age, only half of your emotional energy is available—the positive emotions. With F.E.E.L., this is no longer the case. By shifting from an unconscious, fear-filled state to a more empowered state, you gain the emotional energy formerly suppressed by your negative feelings, which can now support you to make great leaps. It becomes easier to leave your usual comfort zone and finally create the fulfilled life your heart desires. Through this level of consciousness, you learn how to use the energy from your negative emotions to serve you!

WHY THE WORLD IS WAITING FOR YOU TO LEARN HOW TO F.E.E.L.

It is no coincidence that this new way of understanding negative feelings is occurring at this time. You hear the news. I am sure you recognize as much as I do that the world is experiencing major transformations (think political, financial, and environmental shifts, to name a few). You also know that as the world experiences more turmoil, the more people's emotions are aroused. Our world is shifting, and in doing so offers each of us an incredible opportunity to get our acts together.

We've reached a point where, rather than talk about our challenges, we need to take inspired action. This inspired action must come from within. Inspired action is born of love, while frenetic action comes from fear. The simple fact is, we can no longer afford to act from fear, wasting not only the natural resources outside of ourselves, but the considerable resources within ourselves. You and I are needed.

Now more than ever, we must admit that our current understanding of our emotions is *not* impelling us to take inspired action. Persisting in the same techniques to free ourselves from these feelings will no longer get the job done. We need to know how to navigate through these changes, while at the same time not getting caught up in the fear. If you remain in the emotional backwaters, you are going to feel like you are drowning, barely able to keep your head above water.

With the shift in perspective and insight of F.E.E.L., you reassume responsibility for your feelings. You reclaim another layer of empowerment you didn't realize was available to you. Taking responsibility for your emotional well-being means committing to yourself, which I know is no small task. You already likely feel overcommitted. Yet those commitments, which really don't matter in the long run, will dissipate once you commit to yourself. Once you commit to yourself and your emotional well-being, I promise you, life becomes so much easier.

Let me also be clear that F.E.E.L. does not mean you will never feel emotional pain. You still will, but not nearly as much. The day-to-day emotional swings won't happen because you will have learned to get to the core of what is calling for your attention. When a core aspect needs to be addressed and understood through love, the pain is much shorter lived. That's because you will have learned why the emotion is showing up, and how it can serve you. Therefore, the resistance is gone. And the less resistance there is, the more easily you can hear your truth over your fears.

Willing to use your negative feelings as your greatest allies, you'll also be supporting others who are still caught up in fear. As they continue to push and struggle for improvements in their lives, you will be a lodestar to them, showing that another way exists. Even those who have given up on themselves will take notice. You'll be the model of how to reclaim the aspect of themselves that has been shamed, or seen as weak or wrong, and use this energy to support their growth. Reclaimed internal power allows you to attract, allow, and receive, rather than push and try to control. By getting a real F.E.E.L. for your life, you simultaneously demonstrate to others how to flow with the tides of change, rather than row against them. Your negative feelings guide you, provide you with insight, and energize you.

THE SHIFT

Below are the liberating shifts you will experience as you integrate F.E.E.L.

1. You will always experience your emotions. But rather than seeing half of your feelings as enemies, you can now use all of them to energetically fuel your intentions.

2. You reclaim energy, energy that once went into consciously or unconsciously resisting negative feelings. Everything that had locked you in place and weighed you down is now available to further your purpose and full expression of self.

3. You now know the purpose of your negative feelings, and the possibilities they engender. Without these feelings, what would alert you to when you are unconsciously acting from fear rather than love? With this knowingness, you may use your feelings to keep you on track and take leaps that allow your heart to *shine!*

What this means is that now you know how to use your emotions, especially your negative ones, as they were always intended, which is to serve and support your growth. Above all, your negative emotions are there to encourage self-correction by directing awareness to the areas of your life that need your attention. Openness to feelings prevents areas of your life from turning into major problems and causing you deep pain.

Should an area already be causing you pain, you will be shown the way out of that pain and how to shift to long-term well-being. In essence, your emotions want you to shape up your life because when you do, your energy no longer leaks. And the fewer leaks you have, the more energy is available to be of service, feel fulfilled, and live in joy.

Throughout this book, you will see real-life examples (some are composites of clients I've worked with) of how F.E.E.L. has changed every aspect of people's lives. For instance, what is at the core of your finances is also at the core of your relationship issues. Your challenges all show common threads, and your negative feelings are there to help you identify them. Following those threads then leads to an understanding of how fear has unconsciously been driving you. Absent this understanding, you are left to keep chasing away negative feelings and, therefore, continue spinning your wheels.

F.E.E.L. is about revealing the natural support available to you through your emotions that will awaken you to what has remained unconscious (and therefore created unnecessary struggle). I begin Part I by explaining how to shift out of the Emotional Stone Age and into Emotional Awareness. This section of the book shows how and why we remain emotionally stagnant. I share memories of my own futile tail-chasing, before being awakened to F.E.E.L. I then offer a simple breakdown of the F.E.E.L. process into four easy steps that you can apply every time you experience a negative feeling. These steps are so simple that once you get them down, they will click on automatically in your head. You will even find yourself able to skip steps.

But before I detail the shift from feeling to F.E.E.L.ing specific emotions, we'll look at the ego and its fears. This comprises Part II of the book, which is called "Avoiding Emotional Minefields."

It demonstrates how vulnerable we all are to becoming prey of the ego, especially when understanding is limited to fear. True understanding, born of love rather than fear, is shown as the easy antidote to the ego's former tyranny. This insight establishes a core foundation upon which you may apply F.E.E.L. when experiencing a negative feeling.

In the third and final section of the book, I break down all feelings into five main emotions. I call these the "Big Five," because all of the feelings we experience can usually be broken down into one of these five. The Big Five are the most common negative feelings, the ones we tend to struggle with most. They also offer the most specific messages and guidance. Breaking down all emotions into five major leaguers also makes learning how to F.E.E.L. much easier, because you only need to remember what five major feelings mean from the viewpoint of love.

Toward a deeper understanding, I have also included a chapter on over fifty distinct emotions. Once you get the basic processes of the Big Five emotions down, this chapter becomes an emotional reference guide for you. Now, whenever a negative feeling comes up, you have a handy guide to help you remember the true purpose of each specific feeling and how it is trying to shape and support you. Turning to this glossary of emotions will help you to recognize unconscious fears, and shift you back to the higher vibrations of love.

What you hold in your hands is a new framework, giving clear and simple guidance for approaching your emotions from love. Love teaches us to be open. When we are open, we receive. Our negative feelings have been patiently awaiting our ability to see past the illusion of negativity — in whatever we view as negative — and instead recognize the love that pervades all. Should you be willing to open yourself to this approach, you will find a treasure-trove of gifts awaiting you.

The time has come for you to recognize how each and every one of your emotions is your power. **Emotions are the fuel for making your intentions reality.** You can no longer be energized by only half of your emotions. It simply is not working, is it?

When was the last time you remembered that you are magical? When was the last time you acknowledged yourself for the gifts and inspiration you bring to the world? **Emotions are here to remind you of what you came here to do, how your gifts work, and how they are meant to please yourself and others.**

When you learn to consciously choose love over fear, what awaits you is invaluable guidance, love, and support. It is all yours for the asking because you are never, ever alone. This is how you open yourself to truly *shine!*

PART I

EMOTIONAL AWARENESS

SHIFTING OUT OF THE
EMOTIONAL STONE AGE

YOUR NEGATIVE EMOTIONS ARE HERE TO STAY. SOME OF YOU, reading this, may feel your heart sink. Don't worry, this is actually incredible news!

Here's why: If you want to experience your heart shining brightly and fully out in the world where you serve at your highest level, I guarantee you will be challenged by negative feelings, your ego, and fears. It's a simple fact: The more you expand, the more you are going to be hit with emotional blocks inhibiting your progress. (I'll explain more of why this is so in Chapter 4).

I've seen it time and again. You have experienced wonderful successes in your life. Yet, there are one or two areas that you would like to change for the better. The problem is that the strategies you previously used to change your life are no longer effective. You wonder, *Why isn't this working any longer? Why can't I take the next step forward?*

What's happened is that you now need access to more energy to support your progress. The more you try to improve your life, the more challenging the fears and emotional blocks that surface. This means you are advancing on your journey, which is great news!

For this leg of the journey, you will have to acquire new tools that allow you to go deeper than you have previously. What I realized from my own journey, as well as from working with doctors, attorneys, healers, entrepreneurs, stay-at-home moms, and many others, is that the same dynamic is missing from just about everyone. Without it, we cannot shine brilliantly, steadily, or joyously. This missing component is being able to use our emotions from a loving standpoint. I'm talking *all* of our emotions being illuminated by love, rather than fear.

Have no doubt about it — your emotions are your strength! Emotions are the fuel to your creations. You, of course, have been taught just the opposite. You have been led to believe that your negative emotions are problematic and a hindrance. Unaware of these innate gifts, you expend your energy trying to get rid of what will actually support inner peace and growth. Is there any doubt then why you go through bouts of emotional challenges, or maybe even periods of great suffering?

We lost the gift of our feelings when science began to overtake the meaning of our feelings. Interestingly enough, the term psychology comes from the root "psyche," which in Greek means soul. The term psychology was coined in the late 16th century to describe the study and exploration of the soul. Fast-forward a couple of hundred years and psychology is largely employed as a discipline for analyzing the human mind and behavior. The soul component is gone and the mind, where the ego lives and breathes, becomes the sole focus.

By losing the original intent of psychology, we have lost the precious gift to our spirit that our feelings offer. This gift will not be found through the ego, because it comes from the higher vibration of love. We are now being called to an old but new understanding of the foundation of our emotional well-being. Emotional consciousness integrates the gifts of the mind (intellect and ego) along with the spirit (inner wisdom/knowing and love) so that our feelings may serve and support our growth.

Without incorporating the soulful aspects into our emotional well-being, we become lost in a mechanistic jumble of trying to fix, change, or correct aspects of ourselves that aren't broken, just misunderstood. Likewise, a purely spiritual outlook often fails to incorporate the gifts of the mind. The tendency is to push away, "rise above," or somehow distance oneself from those aspects of ourselves that we judge, dislike, or feel uncomfortable experiencing. The time has come to refocus the inner lens through which our current assumptions are made so that we may honor the deeper consciousness and wisdom that resides within us.

THE NEXT STAGE: SHIFTING TO EMOTIONAL CONSCIOUSNESS

Emotional consciousness simply means bringing greater awareness to one's feelings. Through becoming more conscious of your feelings, you can learn to understand all of them from the vibration of love (energy coming from your highest, empowered self) rather than fear (low-vibrational energy). I call this process F.E.E.L., which stands for Feel Every Emotion as Love. F.E.E.L. is the revolutionary way to experience emotions because it enables you to consciously recognize and understand the deeper meaning in all you feel.

One way of visualizing how F.E.E.L. views emotion is through the yin-yang symbol. The yin side is the dark side with light at its core; the yang side is the light side with darkness at its core.

Currently, our understanding of emotional well-being is derived from a yang perspective. This limited understanding begins with the study of psychology, which is rooted in a dominant masculine perspective. From this yang perspective, rational thinking is honored over intuition, and science is honored over spirit. In this paradigm, negative feelings are perceived as problematic and dysfunctional. In other words, an unnatural split was created, classifying emotions as good or bad, right or wrong, healthy or unhealthy. The result is queasy distrust toward one's negative feelings, and disconnection from why you feel the way you do.

Feel Every Emotion as Love reintroduces the yin perspective of our emotions. Reintroduction of yin energy serves to create a more aligned connection between your authentic self (a.k.a. your essence) and your negative feelings. Yin represents the feminine and is seen as the protector of the light. The yin energy teaches how negative feelings may be seen as a source of emotional protection, safeguarding your gifts until you are ready to share them.

Given that women have always been strongly associated with emotions, reintroducing the yin energy back into our feelings makes sense, doesn't it? By learning to view your emotions through feminine energy, you see that at the core of what your ego regards as negative is actually direct guidance. The yin perspective reminds us that in order to feel the peace and fulfillment we desire, we must recognize all aspects of ourselves, no matter how they appear at first blush, as purely love. Feel Every Emotion as Love is a process which provides an understanding of every emotion through love, by integrating and embracing the sacredness of all that we feel. To honor emotions from a feminine understanding is to more deeply understand and work with — rather than trying to overpower, as we have in the past.

YOUR MADNESS BEHIND THE METHOD

When you have a need that isn't being met, you default into unconsciously reacting from anger and fear. We all do. You know you are living in fear when you feel the pain of your emotions more often than you would like. Many don't connect with their fear at all. In fact, they tell themselves that they are doing just fine without a loving companion, or financial security, or a particular life purpose. Whatever it is that is missing from life, they have learned to "adjust" to that lack. Most people have also learned to "keep busy" enough to avoid the negative feelings within. Yet, no matter how lovely life looks and even feels at times, the negative emotion is still there, waiting for its true need to be addressed.

Of course, in the emotional Stone Age, or even the Dark Ages, you don't hear wisdom coming from your negative feelings. You hear self-doubt, confusion, and fear. You hear rumblings that your deepest fears will come true. Your focus ends up being on exactly what you don't want to create, which may eventually make your fears a reality.

The problem is, we don't understand how the negative components of our emotional well-being may serve us. In the emotional Stone Age, our negative feelings, fears, and emotional blocks weigh us down, mess us up, and keep us removed from the life we desire. How emotions are currently understood leads us to one or more of the methods below to handle negative feelings and fears.

1. **Deny, deny, deny.** <u>Your unconscious/subconscious belief is:</u> I refuse to admit anything is wrong because I don't like how I feel and I don't see the point of my negative feelings. All they do is weigh me down.

   You can easily find yourself in denial when you engage in any activity to excess, from eating to Internet surfing, from workaholic to alcoholic behaviors, from shopping (even at thrift stores, if that's your bag) to attending one personal growth workshop after another. You name it — any addictive behavior will keep your feelings at a distance.

Results: Absent any overtly self-destructive behaviors, you are instead unconsciously choosing distractions which inhibit you from fulfilling your deepest desires. Eventually your feelings will come oozing out of you. If you are self-destructive, feelings will usually express in a self-destructive manner as well. If your actions are more about keeping you distracted, your emotions will come out very powerfully, loudly, and with immense pain in order to get your attention away from those distractions. In either case, you usually carry a sense of shame about who you are and what you have become, especially if you feel you are nowhere close to living in alignment with your ideal.

2. **Blame.** Your unconscious/subconscious belief is: It's not my fault for feeling the way I do.

You believe that if others were different you would feel much better than you currently do. You tell yourself if it weren't for my parents being so closed-minded, or my husband being so stubborn, or my children being so oblivious, I would be fine.

Results: Your blame is brilliant, as it keeps your focus on another person rather than yourself. In doing so, you don't have to take responsibility for how you feel. Your feelings are your own, regardless of who may have triggered them. You are the only person who can take responsibility for how you feel. If you continue to blame another, you guarantee your life will not improve. Your blaming makes you the victim and victims are powerless to create change, which will ultimately lead you to depression and/or anxiety.

3. **The positive spin.** Your unconscious/subconscious belief is: I refuse to see what's wrong because I want to focus only on what is good.

   You may spin events and feelings positively because you feel this version of you is what people prefer. You may also use this technique if you are afraid that focusing on the negative will bring more negativity into your life. In either case, you want to experience only the feelings you consider "right" or "positive" by literally pretending the others don't exist. Ultimately, you have generated the positive spin because you're unaware of a healthier, more conscious and authentic choice.

   Results: Your feelings build up in the same ways as in regular old denial. You also feel shame that you still don't feel closer to moving forward, especially since you have worked so hard at remaining positive. You may turn to self-blame and judge yourself for not being optimistic enough as the cause of your emotional problems. Part of your energy remains tied up in shame rather than releasing in the clarity of forward movement along your path.

4. **Release, Clear, Remove.** Your unconscious/subconscious belief is: I recognize how I feel but I still don't like it, as

it is preventing me from being my best self. Therefore, I must get rid of the negative feelings and fear to move forward.

Today, there are hundreds if not thousands of techniques devoted to removing, clearing, releasing, or somehow getting rid of negative feelings. Some can actually provide short-term relief, others not.

Results: Regardless of whether you experience relief or not, what you are missing is the creative purpose of your feelings. Without knowing their purpose, you will continue to experience negative emotions and not recognize these feelings as bearers of guidance and energy to support you. Your focus is on releasing energy that you judge as negative, which could instead be used as energy to propel you forward on your path. These techniques feel fulfilling in the short term because you feel you are "taking care of the problem" by trying to extinguish your negative feelings. But no matter how much you do, you are still caught spinning your wheels in the same paradigm of fear, which will not take you to the fulfilled life you crave.

5. **The Witness.** Your unconscious/subconscious belief is: I witness rather than fall victim to the ego's message of negativity and fear.

   You have found that is better to impassively observe a negative feeling and fear than get caught up in the emotional drama, which is guaranteed to leave you spinning.

   Results: True, you are less likely to get weighed down

by fear when practicing detachment. At the same time, distancing yourself from your negative feelings also means you aren't likely to access their gifts. Remember, each negative feeling has energy that is there for a reason. Rather than detach from negative emotion and therefore its energy, you have an opportunity to utilize this energy being offered to you. Instead of assuming the negative feeling has only to do with the ego's shenanigans, realize there is also a loving energy trying to come through you. Remaining detached means you aren't receptive to feelings' wisdom and power, and only ensures that the same feelings, fears, and emotional blocks will eventually reappear. The Witness *appears to* keep you safe, yet what is really happening is not much of anything beyond an intellectual exercise, resulting in comfy stasis. Rather than distance yourself from this energy, you want to bring it closer to you, to serve and support you.

6. **The Warrior Martyr.** Your unconscious/subconscious belief is: The only way to heal is to sit with my negative feelings and allow them to work through me.

Your strategy is to sink into your negative feelings so that you may eventually come to terms with them, and move on.

Results: I love the Warrior Martyr because you are doing the best you can, given the limited mindset of the emotional Stone-Age. This is where I lived for many years. It works. You do learn, grow, and evolve because eventually you can see your way through the ego's muck and back to your truth. But there is also a lot of suffering in this, especially when critical growth is involved. Unaware of the loving component to your negative feelings, you remain chained to your ego's messages for far too long, with no understanding of why you feel as you do. By practicing F.E.E.L., prolonged suffering is no longer necessary, as you learn to recognize the loving guidance coming through each of your negative feelings.

As you can see from the above examples, each of these commonly used methods has its perks. Otherwise, you wouldn't use them. In the end, however, each exacts a toll, which ultimately hinders your fullest expression of you.

Given the limited understanding you've had to work with, you have done the best you could in handling your negative feelings. There simply hasn't been a perspective that shifts you from "dealing with" your negative feelings to giving you a reason why you would want to love them. This book is finally going to give you the why and how to love your negative feelings. You'll be given the insight to have a healthy relationship, not only with your negative feelings but with all aspects of yourself. You see, you can continue to spend your energy on overcoming, rising above, or freeing yourself from your negative feelings and fears, or you can choose the path of least resistance. The path of least resistance in the long term is to shift your understanding of EVERY part of your emotional self as being perfect to support your evolution.

REFINING YOUR EMOTIONAL LENS TO THE PATH OF LEAST RESISTANCE

I am going to share something with you that is going to blow you away. What you need to understand is that the emotional lens you currently use to see the so-called "negative" components of your emotional well-being is entirely ego-based. Meaning, your unhealthy ego (the false part of you that lures you away from your true desires and ideals) is what is judging your negative feelings as negative! Let me say this again: Your unhealthy ego is what is judging your negative feelings as negative.

"Not true," you are probably saying to yourself. "I don't like how my negative emotions feel. I am the one with judgment against my negative feelings."

The illusion is that *you* are the one at life's helm. (I like to think that I AND God/Higher Source are at the wheel). The reality is that you (or you and God) do have control of your course when you are present and conscious. When you aren't present and conscious, something else is driving your life.

When you are on auto-pilot, of course God/Higher Source is still there; you simply aren't as conscious of that connection. On auto-pi, you are going through the motions, and that is when, unbeknownst to you, your ego takes control. In this state you are more likely to feel threatened that your needs won't be met, because you are no longer listening to your inner wisdom. You're spaced out in the stories your ego has created about the past or the future, making you nowhere near the present.

At this point, your energy is more connected to your ego than your inner truth and wisdom. In other words, this is how you unintentionally get in your own way. Because when your negative feelings signal to you that you are off course, you don't listen to that message. Instead, you listen to what your louder and brassier negative feeling is broadcasting about why you need to feel threatened and scared.

What your ego has done is GENIUS! It knows that if you believe certain emotional signals are "bad news," you will stay busy trying to release, ignore, or deny the natural and helpful elements of those feelings. Even better for your ego is that you are now using methods to avoid or release that which cannot be ignored. We all experience negative feelings from time to time. But when you unconsciously subscribe to the ego's definition of negative feelings, your energy is focused on your fears, not your desires and goals. Now can you see why you cannot really break free of the ego's judgment when you are playing the ego's game?

To break out of the ego's game, an entirely new approach to understanding your negative feelings and fears is necessary. This approach must shift you away from viewing your negative feelings and fears (even the ego itself) from the perspective of your ego. To do this, you'll have to imagine what it would be like to associate your negative feelings and fears with a different meaning beside the one your ego has provided. The meaning your ego so predictably offers weighs you down and pushes you off track. Therefore, the opposite meaning (that is waiting to be recognized by your empowered self) is one in which your negative feelings and fears energize you and keep you on your most fulfilling course.

I'm not talking about sugar-coating your negative feelings, either. Your ego is way too smart to swallow any positive b.s. that you may try to cram down your throat. What I'm seeing coming through your "negative" feelings is guidance that is so completely aligned with your true self that even your ego can't deny its accuracy. What I'm talking about is switching your emotional lens from fear to love.

Switching your viewpoint from "from fear to love" may sound a little hokey for some of you. Yet when I speak about love, I am not talking about rainbows and butterflies. When I speak of love, I am talking about a higher conscious vibration that sees past the illusion of the ego, while at the same time not attempting to sugar-coat reality. This truth-filled love isn't about telling you what you want to hear, or making you falsely believe that everything will be just dandy regardless of how you do or don't act. This love consciousness is present to support you in understanding what needs to change to get you back on track. Neither saccharine nor mean-spirited, the guidance you receive from this higher consciousness is wholly loving, yet clear and straight to the point regarding how you are being called to respond to your life. At this point, you have the choice to respond to the call or engage in the old games of your ego.

There will be those who remain caught up in the addictive fear and intrigue of their ego, and therefore keep playing its game of cat and mouse. The wily ego leads you to believe all manner of falsehoods, including the idea that you are really, really close to ridding yourself of negative feelings and fears, only to find a few hours, days, or weeks later the same type of struggle rearing its ugly head. And *bam!* You are back in the ego's lair and, more important to your ego, again veering off your path.

You can be one who takes a new path to understanding and using your emotions. This is your invitation to choose the path of least resistance. Because when you learn to discern and follow the voice of inner wisdom and love coming through your negative feelings, there will be nothing you need to resist when it comes to how you feel.

SCIENCE AND THE SHIFTS IN OUR EMOTIONAL PARADIGM

"Einstein said that we can't solve a problem while we're at the same level of thinking that created it. Similarly, we can't change a reality if we remain in the same consciousness that made it." (Braden, Gregg, *The Divine Matrix*, p 81.) Emotional intelligence is about questioning the assumptions that have limited our understanding, enabling us to look beyond the distortion of reality that has been created by our conscious and unconscious fears.

A couple of years ago, I was honored to have the opportunity to interview Dr. Larry Dossey. When Dr. Dossey began exploring the field of consciousness back in the 1970s, his colleagues thought he was absolutely crazy. That's because he was viewing consciousness as energy, while his medical colleagues based their view of consciousness on what they'd learned in med school. All were taught — and in most places continue to be taught — that consciousness is limited to a person's brain. Yet Dr. Dossey's research, along with that of a few other trailblazers, revealed that consciousness also exists outside the brain, where consciousness is intertwined and has the ability to impact the seemingly discrete consciousness of all other beings.

The study of consciousness, according to Dossey, "is totally revolutionizing the way we visualize who we are. And medicine is going to be shaken to its very foundations by this process." More than fifty years later, science is finally on Dossey's side. Yet, this information is still not accepted by everyone. Many remain wedded to old ideas, even though the paradigm that they have used is now collapsing.

According to Gregg Braden's best-selling book, *Deep Truth* (2011), "The barrier to more scientists answering the big questions of life and the universe is the constraint of accepting theories based in false assumptions." Emotions are now on the cusp of stirring the same type of revolution by integrating much greater consciousness into our understanding. The false assumption that needs to be teased apart from our negative feelings lies in perceiving those feelings from the limited perspective of our ego's viewpoint.

Even though science hasn't yet recognized the ego's dominance in making assumptions, it has made strides in recognizing how impactful emotions are. Braden's studies led him to the research of Dr. Cleve Backster. Dr. Backster was able to demonstrate just how power-filled feelings are. In fact, his research defied scientific understanding regarding emotions.

In one of his famous studies, Dr. Backster took a sample of DNA from each volunteer he recruited. The volunteer was shown visuals to elicit strong feelings, while her/his sample DNA was held in a separate room. What astounded scientists is that at the exact moment an extreme emotion was experienced by the volunteer, the person's sample DNA in the next room gave an electrical response.

Dr. Backster was so surprised by the results that he decided to repeat the experiment. This time his volunteers were hundreds of miles away from their sample DNA. Again, when emotions were elicited, the DNA was instantaneously affected, even hundreds of miles away! Dr. Backster's work suggests that a previously unrecognized field of energy exists between living tissues through which, sparked by emotion, DNA and cells can communicate . (Braden, Gregg, *The Divine Matrix*, p 46.)

Another important piece of research on emotions was conducted by the Institute of HeartMath.. The studies concluded that positive feelings enhance our DNA, while negative feelings depress DNA, and even cause disease!

Now let's tie in the research of Dr. David Hawkins in his book *Power vs. Force* (2002). His research demonstrated how energy vibrates on a scale of consciousness. Because emotions are energy, they each have a particular vibration. Negative emotions have contracted energy, which is why they vibrate at low frequencies. Positive emotions such as love, joy, and peace on the other hand, vibrate at higher frequencies because they are expansive energies.

Now you may be thinking – Wait, Michelle. All this research you provide — and all the negative emotions that I've suffered – clearly demonstrate that negative feelings aren't at all good for us. Keep in mind, though, that what this research, and your own experience, really show is what happens when we understand our negative feelings exclusively from the ego's point of view. When understanding of our negative feelings is based on fear, they don't serve us, and we contract.

The key here is how science now understands the vibrational energy of emotion and the impact of consciousness on all aspects of life. The two simply need to be united outside the old paradigm that our negative feelings can only be understood in one way. What we stand to gain by integrating consciousness is learning how to live in greater alignment with our highest good, and ultimately being able to serve at our highest level through our emotions.

Dr. Backster's research, in particular, highlights how clearly powerful our emotions are. His research illustrates that emotions are, in fact, more powerful than thoughts, due to their instantaneous impact. Regardless of whether the emotion was positive or negative, the emotion affected DNA, even when over three hundred miles away.

The opportunity that awaits us is in recognizing how ALL of our emotions are a powerhouse in creating change. It is through using both our positive and negative emotions to energetically fuel us that enables us to more readily break through our comfort zones to express ourselves to our fullest ability. We simply haven't been able to access this power because we have been judging that at least half of our energetic fuel is bad!

Did you know that for the space shuttle to break through the Earth's atmosphere, it uses more than 83% of its fuel (Space Shuttle, 2008). Now think about the energy you burn to break through the current habits and beliefs that aren't serving you. Where are you going to find this extra energy to make your breakthrough? Aren't you using every bit of energy you have already?

Although you feel you are utilizing your energy to best serve you, what awaits is an untapped reservoir of energy in your negative emotions. Your ego has simply encouraged you to view and understand half of your emotional energy as being negative. You already know how powerfully *destructive* your negative feelings and fears can be when understood from the ego. What if that same power is available to support rather than harm you? Couldn't you use that extra oomph to move you forward on your path?

You can keep using strategies to overcome your feelings because your understanding of emotions remains limited, or you can learn how to view them from a higher, more expansive vantage point. Viewed through a lens of higher consciousness, all of your feelings provide the guidance, clarity, and support to keep you aligned with your deepest level of fulfillment. They also carry the energy to go above and beyond the limitations of your ego. Will you be at the forefront of this change or will you stay wedded to the ego's notions of negative feelings, fears, and the ego itself? You are now given this new choice and opportunity.

WHY F.E.E.L. MATTERS NOW MORE THAN EVER!

A couple of years ago, I found myself unexpectedly placed in the midst of a profound conversation. After having a fun girlfriend's weekend filled with shopping and relaxing at a spa, I boarded a shuttle to make my way home. Since we had over an hour ride to the airport, people started a conversation about their trips. One had just spoken in Washington, D.C., regarding the welfare of our country. Another was a college professor who taught about the environment. The couple in the back were passionate about buying items made only in the U.S. or that were recycled from second-hand stores/sales. As they spoke, each shared their unique passion on how they would like to see the world change. I sat in amazement at how intelligent and gifted each of these people were, and eagerly tuned in to their deep wisdom. Suddenly, one after another became frustrated as they spoke. Their frustration locked onto how they just couldn't understand how people could seemingly not care about these issues they knew were so critical to the welfare of our country and our world.

Finally I piped up and said, "It's not that people don't care. They do care. What gets in the way of showing they care is their personal pain. When people are struggling with their sense of self, their weight, their relationships, their finances, that is where their attention and energy goes, whether they want it to or not. If you want the world to change, you have to start with the individual, and specifically with the individual's internal world." I then briefly shared how I teach people to love their negative feelings.

Quite honestly, I was surprised by their reaction. What happened was a collective light bulb went off for this van of intellectuals. One by one they shared how meaningful our exchange had been to them. Their sense of frustration turned to smiles because they "got" how everything goes back to how we feel.

I too received a gift. In this moment, these strangers helped me "get" how essential it is for the collective good that we shift our emotions from fear to love. The world simply isn't going to change until collectively we get our acts together. As individuals, we must attend to our energy leaks so that we will have the energy to take the necessary risks in following our hearts and passions. We won't get there by understanding our feelings from fear. We must learn to love ourselves so deeply that we find love in that which we once judged as only negative. **We must be willing to see through the illusions within ourselves before we can do the same in the world.** We can begin by breaking through the illusion of fear in our negative feelings, and recognize the love that reigns supreme! It has been with us all along, waiting for us to open our hearts to its loving guidance.

The importance of understanding the purpose of emotions goes way beyond just you and me. Absolutely, we want to be our fully expressed selves, shining brightly in the world. Each of us deserves that, and learning to recognize the loving guidance in all we feel will get us there.

The bigger picture is this: Forty million American adults suffer with anxiety, and in any given year, almost 20 million Americans experience depression. Given these statistics, I would say there is a problem with the old ego-/fear- based approach to our feelings. When more people are facing anxiety and depression than those who are challenged by cancer, heart disease, or AIDS, don't you think it's time we open to an alternative perspective? As you may guess, anxiety and depression are just the tip of the iceberg; so many others suffer silently from feelings of inadequacy and compromised self-worth that their light seems all but snuffed out. Maybe you are one of them. I was.

What we know from these statistics is that we can no longer hold on to the belief that our current understanding of our feelings is working. I don't pass judgment, as I believe we have been doing the best we could, given the framework we've had. But how many more people need to emotionally flat-line before we determine that a new approach is needed? The new way comes from a higher level of consciousness. It's an awareness that asks us to respond from love rather than react from fear. Although this will take some training, we have much to gain, and lose, when we rise to the occasion.

Below is just a sampling of what we stand to lose by shifting out of fear and raising our emotional consciousness toward love:

WE STAND TO LOSE THE OVERUSE OF PSYCHOTROPIC DRUGS (i.e. Prozac):

- In 2007 doctors wrote 232.7 million prescriptions for antidepressants, making drugs for depression the most highly prescribed medication in the United States. Yet studies have shown psychotropic drugs to be only as effective as a placebo to those with mild to moderate depression. Now even psychiatrists are admitting to prescribing these medications because they feel it is "better than nothing" (Cohen, 2008).

WE STAND TO LOSE THE AMOUNT OF STRESS WE FEEL:

- Emotional distress costs the United States $193 billion annually in lost earnings and 1.3 billion days of lost productivity (Kessler et al, 2008) (Merikangas et al, 2007).

WE STAND TO LOSE FEELING INAUTHENTIC:

- Your choice has hitherto been limited to intentionally focusing on positive emotions and thoughts, or succumbing to the ego's "take" – and hold — on negativity. The results range from feeling shame for natural human emotion to a sense of being out of touch with how you honestly feel.

With F.E.E.L., what we stand to gain is:

STRENGTHENED SELF-ESTEEM:

- Seven in ten girls believe they do not measure up in some way (Real Girls, Real Pressure: A National Report on the State of Self-Esteem, 2008). Girls are not being shown how to value their emotions as strengths. Consequently, they lose connection with their inner wisdom early in life. As girls unconsciously turn away from their inner guidance, they turn instead to comparing themselves to others.

STRENGTHENED RELATIONSHIPS:

- Only one-third of marriages will make it to their 25th

anniversary (U.S. Divorce Statistics, 2002). Blind to the purpose of all our emotions, expressing them in a healthy, loving manner becomes a challenge. And to the degree that we struggle with ourselves against negative feelings, unaware of how they may serve us, we will continue to struggle with others.

STRENGTHENED CONNECTION TO OUR HEALTH:

- 75-90% of all doctor visits are stress-related (Miller & Smith, 2006).
- Emotional distress has been identified as a risk factor in cancer, high blood pressure, cardiovascular disease, and stress-eating (Block et al, 2009). Our inability to connect with all our feelings makes it extremely difficult to connect to the desire to honor our health. There is simply too much disapproval and nonacceptance of ourselves to authentically love ourselves deeply enough to honor our bodies from the inside-out. True health comes from deep love and caring for ourselves from within, a love to which our bodies respond with optimal functioning and balance.

In every part of your life that matters to you, your feelings will be present. Your feelings about yourself determine how you take care of yourself, how effectively you can relate to others, whether or not you feel able to have your needs met, the quality of your job performance, and so much more. Regardless of whether we contribute to the above statistics or not, what is clear is that our current M.O. for handling emotional well-being does not serve the higher good. It does not serve you, and it did not serve me.

I know firsthand what it's like to struggle with issues of self-esteem, and therefore find myself in unhealthy relationships. I also know what happens when mind and body are dishonored, due to feelings of inadequacy. This place of inadequacy led me to be unreasonably hard on myself — even cruel to myself.

Eventually my struggles led me to incredible spiritual awakenings and growth. I experienced therapy, meditation, courses on intuition and spirituality, and women's circles, as well as many kinds of energy healing/releasing sessions and techniques. I wouldn't have changed any of these experiences, as they opened up a whole new world inside of me.

What did not change was that I would still have bouts of sadness, anger, and anxiety (to name but a few). Even though I had truly evolved as a person and had learned so much, I still didn't understand my negative feelings. I'd learned how to temporarily get rid of them, sit with them, or rise above them, yet I still did not "get" them. The tried-and-true techniques that once supported me were now frustrating me! The tools and techniques I had learned as a psychotherapist, life coach, and student of spirituality began to feel inauthentic and problematic. I realized my training had produced but a short-term ruse, providing temporary relief from the aloofness I felt toward my negative feelings. With this realization, I knew my only choice was to give up.

THE PATH TO FINDING A FEMININE
APPROACH TO OUR EMOTIONS

"I AM A FRAUD!" WAS ALL I KEPT HEARING PLAY OVER AND OVER in my head. "How can it be that I receive a degree in clinical psychology, become trained as a life coach, take numerous courses and classes in spiritual growth and evolvement and still not be able to figure out my feelings? And if I can't get why I feel the way I do, what right have I to support others? I give up! I quit!"

That was the out-loud conversation I had with myself in my office several years ago. At that time in my life, I was actually pretty darn happy, believe it or not. I was truly living, especially compared to the emotional suffering I'd experienced throughout most of my twenties that kept me in survival mode. Though I had no clue at the time, this survival mode was about my deep denial of buried anxiety and depression. My feelings were so cleverly disguised behind a façade of smiles and trying to make myself perfect that I did not realize how truly miserable I was. This act of mine became so second nature to me that I'd convinced myself that the internal pain did not exist. When the pain did ooze out, as it always does, I blamed myself for not measuring up in some form or fashion. I was constantly eyeballing myself, asking: Am I burning enough calories? Do my hair and makeup look okay? Is my house clean enough? Is what I just said dumb? Do I usually say the "right" things, laugh enough or share tales that are witty enough? My self-scrutiny was endless and utterly exhausting.

To blow off steam from this engine of self-judgments, and to put my inner critic to rest, I would booze it up! Alcohol was the "perfect" escape from my woes. Drinking felt like a socially acceptable method to decompress from stress. In college, alcohol is the perfect storm of how to deal with stress, pressures, and insecurities. The degree of "fun" seemed to be measured by how much you lost control of your inhibitions. So badly did I want and need to lose control that my drinking periodically went off the deep end. Waking up unsure of just exactly what you said or did the night before is usually not a good sign. Of course, I would be completely humiliated and swear up and down that I'd not drink so heavily ever again. Still, once or twice a year, I would find myself waking up from yet another blackout, filled with shame and worry because I had no idea (or control over) how I'd acted.

When emotions are pent up, we self-destruct. For me, it took getting accepted into a psychology program to recognize that how I was living wasn't working. As I started reading diagnosis and after diagnosis — each one sounding like me! — I decided to go into therapy.

In some ways, I am astonished at how long it took me to realize how miserable I was. In hindsight, I can recognize how easy the game of denial is, even when there's plenty of evidence stacked clearly against you. The evidence is this: Your life isn't going at all as you'd planned. Even after I had to get my stomach pumped in the middle of the night because otherwise I'd have died from alcohol poisoning, I rationalized away my problems. My excuse was that I was a tiny woman trying to knock back as many as everyone else. That is why I lost control.

Doing my own inner work through therapy helped me to finally put an end to my destructive patterns. But even after I made significant shifts in my life and felt quite a bit better, I intrinsically knew that I wanted more than simply to feel good. That is, I knew that I wanted what seemingly few had actually experienced. I wanted to *shine*! I decided to look outside the therapy model to see what else was available. My existential quest for happiness and fulfillment had begun.

BEYOND THERAPY

Breaking free of the therapeutic model led me down an exciting path of reconnecting to my heart, truth, and intuition. Before me was a new landscape of alternative modalities that were all centered on personal growth. Following my heart and what intuitively felt good, I awakened to a path I was born to explore.

That path led me to the teachings of Sonia Choquette in one of her first classes called "Psychic 101." I also partook in numerous shamanic healings and journeys. Meditation, affirmations, and flower essences became parts of my daily practice. I received coaching and became a life coach. My bookshelves were lined with personal and spiritual development self-help books. A new part of me was stirring to life, and I was ready to share this awakening with the world. At last I felt like I was living in alignment with my authentic self.

At this point I was married, had three beautiful children, and was beginning to live my dream job as a life coach. I was thrilled, and felt so much gratitude for how my life was now unfolding. I felt like a new person – well, almost.

THEY DON'T CALL IT A BREAKDOWN FOR NOTHING!

How could it be that I had an incredible husband (truly a partner beyond my dreams), three beautiful, loving children, a deep spiritual connection and a fulfilling career path and still not be completely happy? Though much of my life had come together beautifully, I simply could not understand why sadness, anger, anxiety, fear, jealousy, etc., kept popping up in my life. I asked myself: *What more could I want? What am I doing wrong?* I wondered, *What the heck is wrong with me? If I can't be happy now, I never will be.*

By this time in my life, I had learned to be upfront and open with my emotions. The problem was, I could not for the life of me figure out why certain feelings were still showing up. I had finally succeeded in creating a life filled with many of the gifts my heart so deeply desired. Still, seemingly from out of nowhere, negative feelings would suddenly arise, completely unannounced, and drizzle on my parade.

I religiously wrote in my journal, threw tantrums to release pent-up feelings, and stayed committed to my voice and truth. I tried energy work, emotional release and freedom techniques, self-help guidance, and the Law of Attraction. Some methods helped briefly; others made me sink deeper into my self-inflicted wounds. Soon after a "successful" release, another emotion was sure to come knocking on my heart and soul, trying to get my attention. Law of Attraction work was especially inspiring. At the same time, however, a part of me felt guilty that I'd done something wrong to cause "bad" feelings to show up again and again.

Don't get me wrong. I was and continue to be grateful for the many teachings that lay before me and guided me out from my invisible "walls." I am grateful for how that wisdom, ancient and ever evolving, opened my heart up more and more, giving me moments of tear-filled gratitude. Which is exactly why my negative feelings did not add up. They made no sense at all.

When yet another whopper of a bout with sadness and anger hit me from out of nowhere, I'd had it! My truth was, I felt like a phony. Here I was supposed to be supporting people in their pursuit of happiness, yet my own feelings remained an enigma. After all the training, reading, and learning I had done, both personally and professionally, I still could not figure out why I felt the way I did. "This," I told myself "is *not* okay!"

Rage bubbled up from within me. All the time, energy, and money I had spent, and *still my emotions were getting in my way.* Mind you, we're talking years and hundreds of thousands of dollars for my degree and training. That is when I lost it. Screams bellowed from deep within me. I spat out every curse word I could think of, exorcist-style, as loud as I could. I was in a state of utter disgust that I still didn't "get it" – at all! Flinging myself onto my bed in hot rage, pillows became punching bags. I was convinced, utterly and completely convinced, that there was something fundamentally wrong with me. There had to be! Why else was I not happy by now? I felt like the biggest idiot! I'd bought into all these airy-fairy theories and techniques, only to find myself lost, yet again. I cried, kicked, punched, and launched so many primal screams that I soon became hoarse, and too exhausted to move. Suddenly, I stopped and slowly roused myself from my pillow, which was now covered in snot, slobber, and mascara, and decided to draw myself a nurturing bath. Maybe relaxing in a tub would help bring some closure to my current madness, I thought.

As the tub was filling up with warm water and the sea salts began to dissolve, I thought of one more book I had recently purchased. Hope welled within me. *This is it! This book will give me the answers I need. Everyone is talking about it. Yes, this book will do it!* With a gleam of optimism, I brought the book into the tub. *This will be the one that truly changes me,* I told myself.

Holding on tight to that belief, I opened the book to read. Twenty minutes later, I was throwing that freakin' book against the wall! I let out one last scream. I was done! Another book's theory, right down the tubes. Nothing worked on me. I was a lost cause.

Calmly, I picked myself out of the tub. I decided, right then and there, that I could no longer help others. Who was I to guide others when I was obviously incapable of helping myself? *Just look at me! Who the hell would hire me if they knew how I'd just behaved? Some life coach and therapist I am*!

With a sinking in my heart and in the pit of my stomach, I decided the only thing left for me to do was walk away and let go. Walk away from my passion and my purpose. Walk away from all my training and the only real career I ever knew. Though completely devastated, I still knew that to go on living in integrity, I could not pretend to teach about something I did not understand at its core. Without knowing the purpose of negative feelings, I decided my only choice was to let go.

The one way I knew how to let go was to meditate. So I sat my butt down, as I had hundreds of times before, only this time with the lone intention of seeing how to let go and start anew. I would let go of the hope of ever feeling truly happy, let go of thinking I could support others in their feelings, let go of the person I thought I was born to be. Just let go. Within my heart, I threw up a white flag and surrendered my life to God and the Universal Plan.

After a few minutes in meditation, I heard a voice within me say "You need to write." I responded to that voice: "Write? I already write all the time in my journal." But the voice persisted: "Write on your computer." Why on earth would I do that? I wondered. I hadn't written on my computer since I was in graduate school.

Since the intuitive hit made no sense to my rational mind, I blew off that guidance and went on with my day. The next day, I was awakened at 4:30 in the morning by that same voice saying: "Get up and write." "Now? Are you crazy?" I balked.

Now you must keep in mind that at the time, my daughter was two, and my twin sons were about a month away from turning one. More important, I'd just got them sleeping through the night. Sleep was like gold to me and there was no way I was going to give that up easily. The thought of surrendering my sleep to some crazy voice telling me to write when I had nothing to write about seemed absolutely absurd. For this reason, my inner voice (the voice telling me to go to my computer and write) and my rational mind (the voice that wanted me to sleep) fought for fifteen minutes straight!

Realizing I was getting no sleep at all, I screamed back in my head, *Fine, I will get up and write. But I have nothing to say. This makes zero sense!* Half asleep, I walked down the hallway and sat down at my computer. Whether I was just trying to be a smart-ass or was simply bewildered by the whole event I'm not sure, yet the first words on my screen were "Now what?"

Suddenly, words that were not my own flowed through me onto the computer screen.

Each day for nine months straight, I awoke at exactly 4:30 a.m. (without an alarm clock) and was told to write. I did. Doing so, I still had my doubts. *Why in the world am I wasting my time getting up each morning to write? There is no point to this. I would rather be sleeping.*

At the same time, I knew something extraordinary was happening. There's no denying that whenever I woke up feeling emotionally "off," I found the support I needed in what I wrote. One day in particular stands out because I felt incredibly anxious, yet I was being guided to write about peace. I remember saying, "Write about peace? Are you crazy? I am so far from peace that there's no way I can do that." (At that time, I must have still thought I had something to do with the words I was writing.) That day set me straight. Within an hour, I had gone from feeling anxious to feeling completely at peace. That's because I was given information on how anxiety is set up to bring us back to a core sense of inner peace – and my anxiety was *gone!*

What came through in those wee hours was nothing short of miraculous for me. I'd actually been given the answer to why we feel the way we do. This information did not come from the deep recesses of my brain, nor through any training or reading.. What came through was the answer to my prayers.

It took me about five months of getting up each morning until I realized I might be writing a book. I recognize that five months is an awfully long time to write and not know what I was up to. The thought of writing a book *never* crossed my mind! Plus, if I'd known that was what was happening, my rational mind would have put the kibosh on it right away. After all, I had three children, ages two, one, and one. The last thing I'd believe is that this would be a good time to write a book, or that I even had the capacity to do so.

The whole point of the experience was not just to help me understand emotions from the perspective of love; the experience also revealed another part of my calling. I am also a writer - a notion so far off the scale of reality at the time that I would have never, ever believed it. Me being a writer was a laughable notion to me. Which is exactly why my first book, I did not write. Instead, the words and information came through me to show how my negative feelings were there to tweak the parts of my life where attention was still needed. I was shown that living outside the box is good. To serve at our highest level, each of us must embrace and understand how our negative feelings are guiding us.

My first book is about my journey, and the fine-tuning that had to be made along the way. My next step was to begin sharing what I'd learned with my clients, and witness the dramatic results when negative feelings are honored as their greatest allies. My final step was to create a process based on these teachings so that anyone can learn to love their negative feelings. This process is what I now share with you: how to consciously choose love over fear. Each of us is being called to hear the loving guidance in all that we feel. The more we can do this, the easier and more natural it is to hear the empowered self rather than the fearful self whenever negative feelings arise.

What I was literally awakened to, and have been guided to understand in greater and greater detail, is a perspective about feelings that has changed me to the core. Since those days of waking up at 4:30 a.m., I have learned a whole new way of relating, addressing, and working with feelings.

At last I knew why we feel the way we do, and it is not because:

—we are somehow messed up or wounded,

—we have attracted the negative into our life,

—we were doing something wrong.

There is, rather, a deeper meaning within each of our feelings, fears, and emotional blocks to serve and support us, IF we allow ourselves this gift.

Through the messages and insight I received, the result was a complete paradigm shift in how emotions are understood, related to, and used.

Emotional Paradigm Shift Out of the Emotional Stone Age And Into Emotional Consciousness

PARADIGM SHIFTS TOWARD:	EMOTIONAL STONE AGE:	EMOTIONAL CONSCIOUSNESS:
How Negative Feelings Are Understood:	Negative feelings are a nuisance whose only purpose is to preclude a happy and fulfilled life. They are not understood, only felt as random and confusing.	ALL emotions have a purpose. Negative emotions are present to support you when you have moved away from your highest self, and to help you get back on track.
How You Relate to Negative Emotions:	Irritation, annoyance, and disdain for every negative feeling. You judge your feelings and yourself for how you feel. You want the "bad guys" gone for good!	You feel grateful for how supported you truly are, and for the messages you are now hearing and understanding. It is wonderful to receive guidance rather than remaining stuck. You sense the full integration of every aspect of your being, rather than a warring good-self, bad-self division.

Experience of Emotional Pain:	Varies from mean-spirited to torturous. If you allow yourself to feel your negative emotions, you feel you are sinking in quicksand, and your feelings will swallow you up. Spiraling downward may last for days or longer, with feelings of helplessness as to when your negative feelings will pass. When hit hard, you feel like you are suffocating or drowning in pain.	Varies from laughable to still feeling pain, yet the pain is less and feels more manageable. Now that you are learning to understand your feelings, at times you immediately recognize what the negative feeling was about and move forward. With more deeply felt negative emotions, the ego still rears its head, yet you move more quickly out of its drama because you recognize the alternative meaning that is present to support you. Because you see purpose even when experiencing emotional pain, the pain is neither oppressive nor long-lasting. No longer do you feel emotional suffering.
How Emotions Are Used:	Your emotions use you. You feel no control as to when they'll show up and when they'll leave. Your ego uses your emotions to pull your strings like a marionette and keep you off balance.	Negative emotions are now a helpful tool for identifying fears, beliefs, and thoughts that are not your truth and therefore unproductive. Being able to recognize their loving messages enables you to move more quickly through your emotion and utilize the emotional energy in negative feelings to take action outside of your comfort zone.
Outcome:	You sense that you have hit a glass ceiling and are no longer evolving as you would like. You feel stuck in areas of your life, as if spinning your wheels, and cannot resolve certain core challenges in your life.	You are now accessing energy and feeling momentum that you have never experienced before. Life is now feeling more like an adventure. You feel in ever greater alignment with every aspect of yourself and your life!

As my emotional shift impacted every area of my life, I was able to teach others how to do the same. The most notable shift for everyone I worked with, including myself, is an ever greater deepening of love for oneself. In your heart of hearts, you become thankful for each negative feeling you experience. Rather than feeling bullied or beat up by negative emotions, you feel fully and powerfully loved! You discover the extreme brilliance in how negative feelings have the intelligence and power to propel you beyond what you'd considered possible.

LIVING AN EMOTIONALLY CONSCIOUS LIFE

What always floors me about F.E.E.L. is the way this shift impacts every aspect of life. The force of impact of course makes sense, given that we have feelings regarding everything that truly matters to us. Yet when clients come to me to address one area of their life, I am always fascinated by the way their emotions know exactly how to take them beyond the presenting issue. Their feelings get to the core of how they are living their life out of alignment with their truth in all areas.

First and foremost, F.E.E.L. impacts how you relate to yourself, and therefore how you relate to others. Limitations that once held you back, whether in regard to your career, finances, or relationships, bust open to a scary yet exciting path, one you would never have imagined. Relationships that are aligned with your highest self become stronger, while relationships that you never dreamed could be healed are transformed. You are also able to take care of your physical health at a much deeper level of respect, rather than focus on losing weight, as so many do.

Most important, you trust in yourself at a much deeper level. While other tools have supported you in escaping the proverbial box and becoming visible, F.E.E.L. supports you in taking BOLD LEAPS. Having arrived at a profound sense of trust in the guidance you are receiving, you find yourself comfortably outside of your comfort zone. The result goes beyond a deeper intuitive connection. It is you, all of you, shining brightly in a world of possibility and fulfillment. It becomes clear that whatever you experience emotionally is there to love, guide, and serve your highest good.

Awakening people to this understanding is the Rx for those who have tried everything and are still suffering emotionally. F.E.E.L. also supports healers, therapists, and even energy workers, who recognize how the old paradigm is holding them back (as well as their clients) from greater love consciousness. Regardless of background, the common outcome is greater self-appreciation, honor, and love. Before we are able to F.E.E.L, the ego's blinders stay locked in place. Given a perspective and process that bares the truth in all that you feel, the blinders drop off.

As long as we live, I believe there will always be aspects of ourselves wanting to express more fully and freely. More parts of ourselves that know they can be put to even greater use in serving and loving more boldly. A life-long practice, F.E.E.L. alerts us to when our divine nature needs to let go of elements that once supported us but no longer do. Thanks to our negative feelings, we now have greater guidance to support our journey of full expression and service — even (and especially) when doing so scares us!

Those of you who want to track your progress from the emotional Stone Age to emotional consciousness may download my F.E.E.L. Worksheet for free. Here you will find a checklist for noting each time a negative feeling appears to be supporting a conscious choice of love rather than fear. To download your copy, go to http://www.michellebersell.com/feel-kit/FEELchecklist.pdf

HOW TO F.E.E.L.:

FEEL EVERY EMOTION AS LOVE

YOU DID NOT FIND YOURSELF HERE BY ACCIDENT. YOU ARE HERE because you too yearn to feel more joyful, balanced, and at peace. You long for an inner shift not because you are miserable but because your heart knows you are meant to share more of yourself and you aren't quite doing that yet.

After reading the first couple of chapters, you also now realize that trying to get rid of negative feelings doesn't serve you. At the same time, a part of you is afraid that when you do acknowledge your negative emotions, they will bring you down. You're afraid you will continue to react to these feelings rather than learn to respond from love.

What is great about our negative feelings is how they demonstrate our own mistrust in ourselves. Your mistrust is a throwback to the emotional Stone Age, when you were led to believe you'd done something wrong to cause emotional pain. F.E.E.L. is about restoring trust in your inner wisdom. Through F.E.E.L. you recognize how safe, loved, and free you are just being you, regardless of how you feel.

Now that you acknowledge why making this shift is so essential, let's get to work on the "how to" part. The how is achieved by shifting your understanding of emotions from a contracted, limited perspective to a higher vibratory energy of openness and expansion.

To shift to an expanded viewpoint, we must first address some concepts that are integral to F.E.E.L.

Concept #1: **All of our emotions can be categorized within five core feelings.**

- That is, you can feel a hundred different ways, yet you need only understand these five core messages to realize conscious emotional mastery. I call these five core feelings "The Big 5."

Concept #2: **F.E.E.L. is a four-step process.**

- You will leave emotional dependence on your ego behind and access the more conscious message of your feelings in four discrete steps.

SYNOPSIS OF TERMS YOU NEED TO KNOW BEFORE WE BEGIN

In this chapter, I am simply providing a roadmap of how transformation occurs through F.E.E.L. Let's begin with a brief rundown of what exactly your essence, ego, fears, and the Big 5 mean from a higher-consciousness perspective.

Essence: Essence will refer to your inner wisdom, Spirit, true self, or highest self. This is the essential aspect of you that is all-knowing and all-loving. Your essence is the real, authentic you but is often hidden (partially or entirely) behind your personality, where you feel safer, yet not altogether fulfilled. I also refer to this aspect of you as your empowered self.

Ego: Rather than perceiving your ego as the expression of yourself that you judge, shun, or try to get away from, the ego is understood from a higher-consciousness perspective as a fierce protector. The challenge you will be addressing through F.E.E.L. is to identify those aspects of yourself that your ego blames or shames. Negative feelings indicate an overreliance on, or outdated use of, your ego's protection. From emotional consciousness, you understand that the ego's underlying motive is benign: to prepare you to reclaim more of your authentic self. <u>Fear is simply the language of your ego.</u>

Sadness: Most of the time, we don't understand why we feel sad; we simply don't want to experience the feeling. Sadness is present to express the sense of loss that we carry. Different than grief, sadness is about losing an aspect of ourselves. The loving message within our sadness brings clarity and vitality to how we are meant to reclaim the true self.

Anger: When most people feel anger, they lose control and want to turn outward — "lash out" — with blame or rage. Yet anger, from a higher-consciousness perspective, is a sign that you believe you are powerless in a situation. Your higher self, however, is always aware that you have options to empower and serve you. Your anger is present to show you how to claim your power from love rather than fear.

Anxiety: Anxiety in the emotional Stone Age is a battleground of the mind filled with worry, tension, and scattered energy. From a higher- consciousness vantage point, anxiety indicates your unconscious unwillingness to listen and follow your truth. Your anxiety is present to teach you self-trust, which leads to a core sense of inner peace.

Frustration: There's no emotion quite like frustration to make those "wheels" spin round and round. And you are, quite literally, stuck! The higher- consciousness message of frustration, however, is that you are viewing a situation too narrowly, based upon beliefs rooted in fear. Because you are buying into your fears rather than paying attention to your inner guidance, you are compromising your truth in an attempt to get your needs met. The gift is an inner call to expansion by honoring your truth.

Guilt: From the ego's perspective, guilt is about making you feel bad about who you are as a person. Unfortunately, it works all too well on us. The gift of guilt, however, is to support you in reclaiming the aspects of yourself that have split off or that you have distanced yourself from due to shame. The expanded understanding of guilt lies in claiming a higher version of yourself — one that is stronger and kinder than your ego wants you to believe is possible. The higher-energy vibration of guilt supports your efforts to know and honor your truth unconditionally.

Above is the basis of terms you need to know in order to apply the four steps to F.E.E.L. Just remember that any other negative feelings you may experience can be categorized and assigned to one of the Big 5. For your convenience, in Chapter 11 I provide a list of over fifty feelings as a quick resource to help you recognize their relationship to the Big 5, along with their specific higher-consciousness message. Once you have the Big 5 down, you will be better able to examine whatever you feel, and access the guidance and insight available to you.

FOUR STEPS TO CONSCIOUS F.E.E.L.ING — HOW TO SHIFT FROM FEAR TO LOVE

To shift your energy from fear to your inner truth – which is love — you need a process that makes you conscious of how your ego is triggering you, and the games it is playing. Feeling Every Emotion as Love is this process! By following these four steps, you will be able to call out your ego and consciously choose the guidance of your essence instead. Please read through the steps first before trying this exercise for the first time. The bold portion of the step is what you can return to as your quick reference step once you have gone through the process a couple of times.

STEP 1: IDENTIFY HOW YOU FEEL

Write down all the emotions that are coming up for you. Now see which of the Big 5 is most related to how you feel. If you are feeling more than one of the Big 5, pick the emotion that wants to be addressed first.

It may sound beside the point, but how exactly are you feeling right now? Many of you have it ingrained within that your negative feelings are a downer, problematic, and won't be listened to anyway — so why bother, right? Or maybe you lump these feelings into a huge ball that you call "stress," and you don't go any deeper. In the emotional Stone Age, identifying your negative feelings had no known value because the higher-consciousness purpose of these emotions wasn't being recognized.

With F.E.E.L., your feelings matter, because each one holds specific guidance for you. In other words, there is a reason you feel guilty rather than sad. The reason is that you need the higher-consciousness message of your guilt to guide you forward.

There is no wrong way to identify how you feel. You may be feeling a multitude of feelings at once. Write them all down. See which one feels the strongest OR feels the most fearful for you to address. Work on this feeling first.

If all you get at first is a general sense of stress, that is okay too. Ask yourself what it is like for you to feel stressed. Do you feel sad, frustrated, or angry about being stressed? A part of you doesn't like feeling stressed, and has very definite feelings about the stress you're experiencing.

STEP 2: EGO RELEASE

Allow the ego's version of what you are feeling to come through you. Write down all of your fears, objections, and doubts. You want to be able to clearly identify what your ego is telling you on paper, rather than let the ego's messages continue to run amuck in your head.

This step asks for the reasons you feel the way you do. What has precipitated your feeling this way? Is it work, your spouse, kids, finances? What caused this feeling to get stirred up? Is there someone or something you blame?

The ego's voice is the endless loop you hear in your mind about what is wrong with you (i.e., not good enough). Your ego also conjures seeming facts to justify your feelings (i.e., I am doing the work of two people since they fired my co-worker, so of course I'm stressed).

Write it all down until your ego feels really heard and validated. Sometimes this can be done in fewer than five minutes. If you are working through a core issue, it could take upwards of twenty to thirty minutes. Don't worry! Eventually, you and your ego will get tired of what it has to share.

STEP 3: ACKNOWLEDGE THE GUIDANCE OF YOUR ESSENCE

Now that your ego feels heard, there is space for your inner guidance to come through in your mind. Allow your essence to share the other side of the story, which always differs from your ego's version. What loving guidance or message does your essence want to give you? Give thanks for the information you receive.

Sometimes the guidance is as simple as one word or phrase, which may be all you need. Below are some questions to ask your essence/highest self to stimulate further conversation between you – the administrative you at "headquarters" — and your essence:

A. How does the higher-consciousness message apply to what I am currently feeling?

B. What does my essence want to show or reveal to me?

C. What does my essence want me to know specifically?

D. What vision is my essence holding for me?

*If you are feeling challenged connecting to your essence, go to http://www.michellebersell.com/html/innerdialogue.mp3 to download the meditation, or go to Appendix A to read the meditation yourself.

STEP 4: CLAIM AND ACTIVATE YOUR NEXT STEP

A. **Ask your essence what single step would bring you into closer alignment with your truth.**

B. **Commit to a date by which you've demonstrated that step through an actionable measure.**

If you feel uncertain as to what this next step is, use the Inner Dialogue Exercise in Appendix B. This exercise enables you to strengthen your relationship with your essence if your energy has been unconsciously aligned with your ego. The more you practice listening to your essence and acting on its guidance, the stronger your relationship becomes. The Inner Dialogue Exercise will provide you with details on how this is done.

REMOVING EMOTIONAL STONE AGE BARRIERS

F.E.E.L. relies on the four-step process to successfully elevate your feelings from a limited ego perspective to one of higher consciousness or empowered self. To ensure success, you want to address all objections or concerns you may have. Below are a few of the most common. If you have others, be certain to take time to write them out as in Step #2 of the F.E.E.L. process.

Common concerns:

- Will this work for me?
- Will I be able to apply these steps at the actual moment I experience a negative feeling?
- Will applying F.E.E.L. be difficult to do?

All of the above questions need to be addressed. You see, if even one of these questions lingers within you, your ego's got you trapped in its game. Ego will trot out these doubts to keep you from making F.E.E.L. your way of life, even though you are being guided to make this shift. Your ego is a master at keeping you resistant to change. Let's cover these questions now and put your ego's fears to rest so you can keep moving forward!

After years of trying to fix and remove certain feelings, the greatest concern is often: "Will the F.E.E.L. process work for me?" Your answer is actually found within your fear. Your fear is that you don't want to risk disappointment and waste any more time and energy. Your reality is that you have likely spent many years trying to fix, remove, or otherwise improve how you feel.

F.E.E.L. does not perpetuate this cycle. F.E.E.L. fosters acceptance of how you feel and in doing so, recognizes the duality in all your emotions. F.E.E.L. never tells you to feel any different than you do. There is information, guidance, and clarity to be gained in all that you feel! If you have not previously realized or been able to recognize the gifts within all that you feel, this process is for you!

Obviously, if you can't get out of bed to attend to your daily life, this process isn't for you — yet. Whatever the case, messages from your empowered self still apply. But if you are experiencing a high degree of emotional pain, chances are you won't be able to access insight from higher consciousness without additional one-on-one support. Fortunately, incorporating F.E.E.L. into any method of support only enhances your opportunity to grow. F.E.E.L. is a perspective and process you will carry with you for the rest of your life. It never fails to bring deeper understanding of your truth, needs, and desires.

This process also isn't for you if you don't want to feel your feelings. Here's the deal with F.E.E.L.: It is not about trying to take away your negative feelings. One of my favorite authors, Brené Brown, Ph.D., stresses that we can't selectively block off certain emotions. It doesn't work that way. Repressing or suppressing one emotion will, because it's linked to all the other feelings, also block the so-called "positive emotions," the ones you'd like to feel more often. More importantly, *you need your negative feelings* to alert you to when you are acting from your ego. F.E.E.L. shortens the length of time you feel emotional pain, sometimes causing shifts within seconds. IF you are willing to act upon your inner guidance, it eliminates the need for emotional suffering. When you act upon this guidance, your negative feeling has done its job to alert and guide you. Without you trying to quash your negative feeling, the emotion dissipates on its own. Better yet, you find satisfying resolution to your challenge. Rather than a quick fix, where you eventually end up back where you started, the issue is truly resolved.

By following the four steps to F.E.E.L., you will be on your way to shifting out of the lower vibration of fear to love. At the same time, there really is no such thing as following the steps in the "right" way. Emotional consciousness simply illuminates the dynamics of following the demands of ego or the loving guidance of highest self.

And guess what? Sometimes you will choose your ego! You'll want to attend that pity party from time to time. That's okay. Just try to choose your ego consciously. When you do, you won't stay very long at the pity party (and blame blast). Imbibing the very same whine wine and dancing to the all-too-familiar ego-ditties becomes a real bore! You are now too aware of the ego's games for them to engage you for very long.

Therefore, *DON'T get caught up in any perceived failures or shortcomings, even if you are following the steps to a "T."* Your aim is simply to become conscious of your choices when it comes to how you feel. As you begin to open to how the messages from your empowered self are supporting you, the steps will easily unfold and you'll realize how the insight applies to your current experience. What I've seen time and again is that all it takes is one time where the process reveals the guidance you need and you are hooked! You will use this same process over and over throughout your life to get the clarity you need whenever you are experiencing an uncomfortable feeling or fear.

It takes practice, and a bit of faith, to learn it is safe to let go of your constant companion, fear, and instead choose to trust your empowered self's message. The more you use F.E.E.L., the easier the process becomes. After some practice, you will be able to apply the steps in your head while experiencing a negative feeling.

Then you'll find yourself barely needing or not at all needing to go into the ego's interpretations. F.E.E.L. makes you so aware of your ego's stories that they no longer have the same impact. At first, these old stories will become annoying, then boring, and finally forgotten because you are responding more often from love rather than fear.

For the first few weeks, stick with writing out on paper your responses to the four steps. Seeing what you write spotlights the ego's way of pushing your buttons and exposes the fear messages it repeatedly instills in you. Then one day, that same message that was triggering a downward spiral becomes your signal that what you are hearing is simply not true. All at once, you will know what your highest self is guiding you to do, and the ego's old boring story will be history!

Typically, the less emotional pain you experience, the quicker you will recognize how a message from higher consciousness is guiding you. If you are in deep emotional pain, go back to writing out the steps. Occasionally, you will have an "emotional orgasm" (mmm...Now doesn't that sound intriguing?). Emotional orgasms occur when initially, the ego's version of the feeling holds sway, but then, during that intense expression, you "get" the higher-consciousness message and instantly shift to ecstatic joy! This isn't the norm, but it sure is fun when it happens!!

I cannot overemphasize the enormity of what you'll be doing for your emotional well-being by learning how to F.E.E.L. You are retraining decades' worth of fear-based understandings and reactions. *Doing so will take conscious effort because emotional consciousness is by no means a quick-fix placebo.*

I'll be upfront — F.E.E.L. will challenge you. You won't always want to do what your inner guidance is telling you. It may feel uncomfortable and at times even frightening. Yet by learning to attune to your deep inner wisdom through your negative feelings, you will gain greater trust to take leaps when you are called to do so. Ultimately, this is exactly how you learn to SHINE.

Ultimately, F.E.E.L. means less struggle, greater room for expansive feelings, and increasingly greater alignment with your highest version of you. Aspects of life that provoke the strongest feelings in you also hold the greatest meaning for you. Being able to recognize and address your negative feelings from an empowered perspective, therefore, has a significant positive impact on everything that matters to you most. The result is continuous energetic waves of emotion flowing within you to support your fullest, brightest, most authentic expression of self.

Certainly, you will face inner storms from time to time. F.E.E.L. shows you how to ride out those storms while remaining connected to a sense of inner peace. Through this process you are accessing an energetic current that constantly reminds you of how very much cared for, safe, and guided you are. Flowing into the mighty sea of life, your heart is at peace. Rather than drowning in your negative emotions, they now become your lifesaver to bring you back to your brilliance. All you have to do now is choose: sink, by remaining tied to an ego-based version of your feelings, or swim, by learning how to apply F.E.E.L. to your life.

PART II

MINEFIELDS: UNDERSTANDING AND LOVING YOUR EGO AND FEARS

UNDERSTANDING YOUR
EGO THROUGH LOVE

"I AM SO FED UP," SANDRA SHARED AS SHE FIRST SAT DOWN with me. "I have talent, I have more to share with the world, yet I can't move forward in my business. What is going on here, Michelle?" I replied, "It's your ego, Sandra." She asked, "Okay, well, can you help me get rid of it?" "No, I am sorry." Sandra didn't like that answer! "Why on earth not?" My answer was simple, "Because you need your ego, Sandra."

Have no doubt about it, your ego is the source of your pain. Your ego is the reason you find yourself stuck, lost, empty, or confused. Your ego is the anchor that weighs you down. If you find yourself knowing there is more to your life, yet you can't seem to make that vision your reality, your ego is to blame.

Your ego is usually successful at taking you off course because its unhealthy aspect, otherwise known as your Shadow, is running your life and you don't even know it's happening. Unbeknownst to you, you are buying into it and living your life trying to prove your unhealthy ego is absolutely correct about the kind of person you are. Needless to say, the type of person your unhealthy ego would have you be is seriously lacking! Your unconscious response is to shame those aspects of yourself your ego judges.

Because of this judgment and shame, you want to run as fast as you can from your relentlessly pursuing Shadow. You believe you would be a much better person if you didn't have this hindrance in your life. All you want to do is get rid of your ego and get back to truly living, right? Not so fast! When your goal is to break connection with your ego, guess who's at work? Your ego is! And who's casting that Shadow? You are!

Thinking you'll be a better person after you get rid of your ego is the same as believing you'll feel better about yourself when you are more successful, lose weight, behave more lovingly, etc. Your ego is always the messenger of your not being good enough. What an ingenious way to have you think you are not enough by telling you to get rid of a part of yourself that you cannot! This guarantees you will continue to chase your tail.

Regardless of how your ego has you spinning, you can move past its limitations. To do so, *you must stop trying to rid yourself of or distance yourself from it.* When ego is understood through this distorted lens, you unconsciously remain in a state of resistance toward YOURSELF! Remember what world-renowned psychiatrist Carl Jung stated: "What you resist, persists." What you are resisting is what you judge about yourself. Instead, why not shift from judgment to love and see how your ego actually serves you?

Throughout all of your life, you are meant to grow and evolve into the highest version of yourself. With each step you take to realize more of your potential, you will encounter your ego attempting to hold you back. What this means is that even if you aren't consumed by your ego, there are still limiting beliefs about yourself that linger, even in the most consciously evolved.

Through emotional consciousness, you begin to understand how your ego can serve and support you, even when it seems to be doing the exact opposite! You see, your ego's job is to protect your essence. Only you can determine when your essence no longer needs the same degree of protection.

WHY THE EGO EXISTS

Without your ego, you would have found it extremely difficult to survive up until now.

Even if you feel you were well taken care of growing up, you were bound to experience disappointment. No one can constantly ensure that all your needs will be met in every given moment you experience. As a child, you don't have much, if any, control regarding your circumstances. Your essence needs and deserves protection when you don't have any choice as to how or if your needs will be met. This is where your ego steps in to support you.

Your essence desires to feel safe and loved. There were likely times when you felt it wasn't safe to show your true self. When you don't feel loved or accepted for who you are, you want to be protected from that pain. Your ego's job is to protect you from the pain of those unmet needs so that you can keep on functioning. Your ego does this by creating an ingenious system of protection called the false self. **Your false self is what enables you to accommodate to less than optimal circumstances while attempting to get your needs met the best way possible, regardless of your environment.**

At times, your false self will even convince you that you do not have certain needs. The protection offered by this false self helps you to continue progressing as well as you can when conditions are difficult. When refashioning your authentic self to get your needs met doesn't work, your false self supports you in putting up protective walls. You can now more easily ignore or deny your unfulfilled needs and desires. Thus immured, you are not consciously aware of what your true inner needs are because they were made inaccessible by shame and judgment, which your false self needs for its survival.

Your ego goes to all this trouble is to prevent you from becoming hopeless. Hopelessness means you lose your spark, your desire to fully live. Your ego's job is to protect your essence from ever reaching that point. In other words, **your ego is a sacred protector of your authentic self.** Tirelessly your ego stays at your side, to whatever degree necessary, until you are willing to claim, honor, and appreciate all aspects of your truth.

WHY YOU STRUGGLE WITH YOUR EGO

The reason you feel challenged by your ego is because your false self was designed only for *temporary* protection. Unfortunately, you tend to grow used to the protection of the false self because this version of you feels safer than exposing the "real" you. Thanks to your false self, all those aspects of yourself that you judge and are ashamed of get to be hidden from your consciousness. Now who wouldn't want that? Of course, you're going to hang on to your false self if it means those "ugly" parts stay hidden!

The problem is, when you rely on your false self for protection, you inhibit the full expression of your essence. In fact, the more you need your false self for protection, the more you grow accustomed to this impostor, mistaking it for your true self. Even worse, you start to believe your false self is the self that others prefer. Once this happens, you begin to whole-heartedly believe you could not get your needs met without the "winsome" ways of your false self.

Because the false self seems much easier for others to love, you determine there is something not quite right about your authentic self. Your authentic self is seen as more and more inadequate, while your false self appears to be the only way to be validated. In turn, you invest more and more energy into being this version of you that isn't true.

Inevitably, the illusory protection of the false self brings pain. That's because your false self will never be able to support you in creating the authentic life you really want. Your false self is a great short-term strategy for protection, yet one that comes with the cost of losing connection to your true self.

When you begin to recognize this cost, you realize you have two choices:

1. Continue to allow your false self to run your life, offering protection from what feels shameful.

2. Choose your authentic self, regardless of the costs.

In the short term, choice #1 seems a lot easier, yet it comes with great pain. The pain occurs because choosing your false self over your inner wisdom means detachment from your authentic self. The emotional pain can only worsen the more you detach yourself from your inner wisdom. The result is an internal aching for your life to be and feel different.

Choosing option #2 can feel very challenging in the short term. More often than not, choosing your authentic self over all else feels as if you are losing any chance of realizing your deepest desires. Yet, when you decide to let your essence guide you, your authentic self becomes more and more empowered, while your false self recedes.

The reality is that you are learning to identify and honor your true needs at a much deeper level than you previously had, rather than trying to manipulate the external to meet your needs for you. Learning to meet your own needs is definitely easier said than done, because your ego is such a master manipulator. In fact, the more consciously evolved you are, the trickier your ego becomes. To get to the point where you are able to consciously choose your authentic self over your false self, you must first become aware of what your false self is trying to hide.

BRINGING YOUR SHAME TO THE SURFACE

At some point, you determined there were parts of yourself that were unacceptable, and so you buried them deep within you. You judge these aspects of yourself as inadequate, and unacceptable to those who would otherwise love and respect you. You don't want others to know these parts exist. Because you think they are innate flaws, you believe they are impossible to change. You should know! You've tried over and over to fix, get rid of, or suppress these "imperfections," only to fail. Common shame refrains include (but are not limited to) feeling:

- Not good enough
- Unlovable
- Undeserving
- Incompetent
- Useless
- Worthless
- Not smart enough
- Too needy
- Selfish

Your shame refrains are what you are unconsciously fighting against all the time. You battle these feelings because you fear they may define the real you. Rejecting these seemingly undesirable aspects, you unconsciously devote your energy to proving them wrong. Unbeknownst to you, your goal is to demonstrate that you are not that which you unconsciously judge yourself to be — wrong, inappropriate, or not good.

You try not to be too needy by being independent. You try to avoid selfishness by showing care for others. You try to win deservingness by working really hard. The problem is that when you unconsciously try to cover up "faults," all your efforts toward independence, caring, or working hard are somehow "off" – contaminated and confused by the false premise upon which they rest. And that false premise is that there is something wrong with you! The result is that this delusion ultimately works to your detriment. All this covering up has resulted in the loss of your authentic self and, all too often, becoming that which you most feared (i.e., selfish or needy).

Your energy has unconsciously gone into hiding and protecting that which you judge and feel ashamed about, rather than living in alignment with your true self. Lost to defense, this vital energy could otherwise have been used joyously and creatively. But the good news is that as you continue to live misaligned with your highest self, negative feelings will show up and prod you make the necessary changes.

Your negative feelings are present to wake you up from your ego illusions and show how every aspect of yourself serves a purpose. In other words, there is a higher benefit to that which you find shameful. It is only when you make those aspects of yourself "wrong" that they leak out and express in distorted ways that don't serve you. As you reintegrate those qualities you once rejected, your authentic self becomes more empowered. You're no longer hiding, which means your energy is freed to serve your highest expression of yourself.

To integrate the themes of shame that you carry, ask yourself the following:

1. How does my shame impact the way I currently live?
2. What would be different about how I live if I weren't trying to prove my shame wrong?
3. What would it mean for me to hold both my theme of shame, and its opposite, as aspects of the real me?

To be able to accept a part of yourself that you judge, all you need to do is recognize how that aspect of yourself has served you. For instance, if you judge yourself as selfish, how has being selfish served you? Or if you judge yourself as a coward, how has being a coward served you? From the higher consciousness and vibration of love, you need every aspect within your being. Selfishness encourages you to take the time to care for yourself. Being a coward impels you to reach out for support while you build up your inner strength. Healing occurs when you recognize how every aspect of yourself carries at its core a gift, when expressed from love rather than fear.

You can safely surrender to your ego by closely attending to what your false self is telling you. Your ego protects only that which seems shameful. The duality within each of us is what makes us human. You have both sides for a reason. By disowning aspects of yourself, you force the rejected quality to go underground, where it finds ways to unconsciously sabotage you so that its needs will be met. Accepting and honoring the duality of your being allows each quality to function in a healthy and honest manner. Not only do they serve to illuminate you with insight and peace from within, but also to *shine* outwardly, into the outside world!

YOUR EGO, THE MASTER MANIPULATOR

As I mentioned above, being on this path to consciousness does not give anyone a hall pass that diverts them from ego's manipulation, including me. Through all my experiences in assisting people to work with their ego, I never cease to be amazed at how tricky the ego can be. In fact, the more consciously evolved you are, the more conniving your ego is! It behaves this way because it has suffered heavy "loses" – that is, numerous protective layers of falseness have been stripped away. Now it must up the ante to maintain the status quo. This means it will be sneaky, finding ever subtler ways to keep you stuck.

For instance, a few years back, when I wrote my first book *Emotional Abundance: Become Empowered,* I felt completely open to the possibilities of life. I was proud of the risk I had taken in waking up at 4:30 a.m. and trusting my inner guidance to write, even though I had no idea doing so would lead to a book. The risk paid off immensely, as the book afforded me national media coverage and expanded my work internationally. Yet after the initial buzz subsided, I wasn't sure what I was supposed to do to get the word out further. I kept telling myself: *I am a psychotherapist and author, not a marketer. If this book is meant to sell, it will. I put this into God's hands.*

Does the phrase "putting my book into God's hands" sound like the ego to you? It didn't to me. It sounded like trust and faith, qualities I should be trying to develop on my journey. For a while, I believed the pretty message I was telling myself too. Fortunately, my emotions came into play, indicating there was more beneath the surface.

It was an ordinary morning and I was getting dressed. I was in a good mood, yet a part of me felt hesitant to start my workday. As I thought for a moment about what the hesitancy might be about, there was *a small sense of frustration* (a key to deeper understanding through love!). I truly believed in my heart that more people were eager to learn healthier ways to understand their feelings. The problem was that I had no idea what to do to effect this outcome. I remained trusting in the Divine's power, but at the same time saying that I *entirely* give this over to God no longer felt right to me internally.

Suddenly, as I was figuring out what necklace to put on, the old adage occurred to me: "God helps those who help themselves!" I then realized the deeper meaning. I needed to take action toward helping the word get out more.

Now here is the brilliance: My ego's message completely served me while I was unwilling to take action — until I became willing! Truth be told, after writing the book and figuring out the publishing world, I was worn out. Learning to market my book felt like a whole new education I would have to undertake and I did not feel like taking on another role. My ego graciously stepped in to suggest that marketing was not my place, leaving me to feel justified in my inaction.

Through a hidden sense of frustration, however, I was able to see my ego at work. That morning, getting ready, I "came out" as a closeted victim. Finally, I was ready to see! What I saw was someone holding on tight to an identity (psychotherapist and author) because I was entirely unwilling to expand at that time. Without my even realizing it, I'd become the helpless author who didn't know how to spread her message. From this perspective, I was powerless, as victims always are.

What you must remember is that being the victim is comfortable to all of us at some level. When you are in victim mode, you get to affirm and invigorate your shame themes. Because we are so familiar with these themes, they can be much more comforting than being fully exposed, owning our full power to accept responsibility, and allowing ourselves to *shine*.

For me, not being able to get my message "out there" fit in quite well with my shame themes of not being good enough, deserving, smart enough, etc. In fact, these themes are so unconscious and yet comfortable that I had *no idea* they were playing out in my life. So it wasn't until I felt a negative feeling that I woke up to how I was being played by my ego.

When I realized how tricky my ego had been in having me play the victim unawares, I had to laugh! I could not believe how good my ego was. (Seriously! And I teach this stuff!) Fortunately, I knew how to listen to my frustration from love, and subsequently use the Four Steps to Emotional Consciousness to understand my ego in action. If it weren't for understanding the loving guidance in my frustration, I would have remained in the dark, unaware of my ego's expert manipulations!

What I am most in awe about from using this process is how accurate feelings are. I didn't feel frustration until I was ready to move forward. When my essence could access the energy to take the next step, my feelings guided me to greater clarity — as well as the action I needed to take. Through understanding frustration from the higher consciousness level of love, I could see my ego at play and understand what my next step needed to be.

Since I don't care for consciously being the victim, it was easy for me to take the necessary steps toward greater empowerment. Of course, there were still fear and doubts along the way. But these were the tests I had to go through before my ego could feel sure I was ready to release the safety of my victim story.

The truth of the matter is that my book was safely in God's hands and remained there until I was willing to do my part. This nudging from the Divine came through my seemingly negative feeling, frustration, telling me that my faith was now being used by my ego as an excuse for stasis. In other words, my book was still in God's hands, but now God was coming through to say, "Faith alone is not enough. You need (and are ready) to take action!"

Understanding my frustration from love allowed me to step out of my limited view of the self I defined as "psychotherapist and author" and embrace the business side to my work. Although this new role felt overwhelming to me, I felt empowered and inspired to take steps to promote my work. With genuine gratitude I said to my ego, "Thank you for protecting me until I was ready to claim more of my power and potential." I meant every word!

Through working with my ego, I opened myself to new possibilities and claimed even more of my personal power. My work expanded in ways I would have never foreseen, allowing me to work with other well-known experts in the field of consciousness and personal growth. The results have allowed me to refine my work to more clearly support others with their negative feelings, fears, and ego through love! Ultimately, because I was able to see my ego through the eyes of love, my ego loosened its tight grip.

THE EGO RELINQUISHES POWER ONCE YOU RECLAIM YOURS.

Nothing affirms your power over the messages of your false self more effectively than authentic gratitude and love for a job well done by your ego in trying to keep you safe until you are ready to soar again!

WORKING WITH YOUR EGO TO EVOLVE — SHIFTING TO EMOTIONAL CONSCIOUSNESS

In the emotional Stone Age, when people realize that their ego is impeding their desires, they make it the villain. Making your ego the villain, only puts you in resistance mode and ultimately makes your ego stronger. Fortunately, you now can see your ego through the lens of love, which ignites a desire to understand how your ego serves you.

Since ego's job is to protect you, your job, from a higher-consciousness perspective, is to thoroughly recognize what makes you feel vulnerable about your authentic self. Remember, the ego protects only what you judge as too alarming or unflattering to be seen within you. Through recognizing what feels vulnerable within you, you can discover your ego's motives and work with it to serve you!

It's important to remember that your ego, as your protector, does not want to risk getting your essence hurt. Your ego's job is to determine when you are truly ready to embrace more of your true self. Your work is to demonstrate to your ego that you are indeed ready to recognize and accept aspects of yourself you have denied.

Let me be clear: Simply affirming your acceptance is not enough for your ego to loosen its hold on you. This could be likened to a parent handing over the car keys to a child who has never driven, simply because the child says they're ready. You would be setting your child up (and others s/he encounters) for disaster. Just as you know better as a parent, your ego knows better as your protector. Its job is to carefully prepare you to be able to handle all that comes with your deepest desires.

Your ego's inner work, from the perspective of higher consciousness, is to ensure you are ready to honor your life's calling. This means preparing your inner self for both the perks, as well as challenges, which may come with greater success. Let's say, for example, that you tell yourself, your loved ones, or God/Universe that you stand ready for your next level of expression. What most of us mean by this is that we are ready for the positives, such as more rewarding work and an increase in pay. But are you also ready for the challenges that come with success? Do you feel adequately prepared to take uncomfortable risks, or handle those who criticize your work? Claiming you are ready to grow does not necessarily mean that you are ready. Are you also prepared to face your uncertainties, areas of ignorance, fears, and self-doubts?

Your ego will offer you *myriad opportunities* to either remain at your current level of awareness, or expand. Ingeniously, these opportunities are not always directly related to the area in which you are attempting to evolve. In other words, if you want to express more of your potential in one area of your life, your inner preparation is likely to take you in a completely different direction.

Time and again, people have come to me for support with one particular issue only to find out how it is tied to another. Examples include not being able to lose weight — linked to unhealthy relationship boundaries and low self-worth; an inability to make more money — related to relationship problems; and impotence — tied to unwillingness to take on more personal responsibility. The list could go on and on. Which is why weight-loss/health is more than just diet and exercise, and building wealth is more than working hard and making smart decisions. In every area of life that matters, your emotions are there guiding you to live your most fulfilled life.

My client Sonja is a great example of how ego is present to transform people in ways they least expect. Sonja was ready for her next level of success. She wanted to share her gifts with the world and make more money doing so. Yet, no matter what Sonja did, she couldn't seem to take her business to her next level of potential. Although her work was going well, she needed her work to go better financially.

Due to the financial struggles Sonja was facing, she also found herself fighting more with her husband. Deep down, she wanted more support. But when Sonja spoke up, she felt it really didn't do any good, as "her talks" always hurt her husband's feelings. In the end, nothing got resolved or changed.

Since her feelings regarding her husband were really charged, we started there. The core emotion she was feeling was anger. Anger, as described in Chapter 7, is about claiming more of your power. In Sonja's mind, however, she was already comfortable in her power. (This is the delusion that ego creates, yet her feelings were telling me otherwise.)

I asked her to go over a recent argument. Even though Sonja was speaking her mind, I could tell there was a hint of apology in how she spoke to her husband. I asked her, "What are you afraid would happen if you were to fully share your truth and own it without apology? That he'd leave you, your marriage would be ruined — what is it?" Sonja responded, "My marriage would be in disarray." I lovingly and honestly shared, "It already is. Your fear is already your reality." Her ego was trying to protect her from the truth of her reality.

I continued, "What your angry feelings are trying to do is support you in getting out of this mess by teaching you how to lovingly stand in your power and truth. Getting comfortable with lovingly standing in your power and truth is also exactly what your business needs to take it to the next level."

Sonja felt as if the blinders had been removed and she could now see how marital tensions were present to support her growth.. Knowing this, she began utilizing her anger from a place of love to live in greater integrity and power unapologetically. Doing so made a light bulb go off for her husband, who could suddenly see how she was supporting their marriage. What Sonja learned at a deep level is how her emotions were supporting her to move past old safety nets created by her ego so that she could more fully claim her potential. Behind everything you want to change is your ego. On the surface, your manipulative ego blinds you to the crux of the problem. This is how it keeps you safe and protected. Yet for those of you who want to evolve beyond the ego's limitations, negative feelings are your guide to help you see what your ego doesn't want you to see.

Your negative feelings indicate that something is not working for you. By understanding the loving message coming through your negative feelings, you you gain the key that unlocks the bars of protection formed by your ego. Rather than define aspects of your life from behind these bars, the door opens for you to recognize exactly how you are being called to own more of your truth, love and potential. This is when your perspective shifts from your ego inhibiting your progress to your ego supporting your evolution and growth.

The great news is, even when you fall back on your ego from time to time, you are still able to grow and evolve. In fact, right before you are ready to take your big leap in a certain area of your life, you're apt to fall one more time under the ego's spell, to hide within its stifling cell. But with this final "fall" comes the conviction that you will be able to tolerate the uncertainty of "how you will land" when following your inner guidance. It becomes clear that daring action always beats the pain of your ego's limitations.

The objective of emotional consciousness is for you to learn each time you choose your ego. At first, you won't be aware that you chose your ego. Only afterwards will you see how you got caught in your ego's story. By remaining conscious, you start to look at what got you pulled in, what fear was triggered, and how you in turn reacted rather than responded. This information is GOLDEN, because you are now aware of what you judge what makes you feel shame. The more aware you become, the more you have a choice to choose love over fear.

SURRENDERING TO YOUR EGO

Love is about surrender, rather than fighting. By not living in the complete wholeness of who you are, energy that could be going to creating an even more fulfilled life is wasted on your ego's judgments. Through conscious integration, your ego recognizes you no longer need that degree of protection and further lets go of its hold! The result is that energy — once used to hide your true, whole, and full self — is now available to further support you in fulfilling your life's work! The more you can see how your ego is trying to prepare you to claim more of your gifts, the more you can reclaim your internal power.

An integral aspect of me being able to finish this book was accepting the notion that I am not good enough, as well as that I don't matter. Sounds awful, right? Here's why loving these insecurities in ourselves is crucial. When I did not accept not being good enough and not mattering, my energy was going toward trying to prove I was good enough, and that I mattered. Unconsciously, I was trying to prove this through writing a stellar book. Yet, with those unconscious shadows riding my ass constantly, I was never freed up enough to write from my heart. My ego kept telling me my writing wasn't good enough and no one really cared to examine their feelings, etc...I would then end up focusing my energies on other aspects of my work and blow off writing, which of course frustrated and saddened me.

What I realized was that these shadow parts of myself, the sides of myself I would feel so ashamed for anyone to know existed in me, had needs. The shadow parts wanted to be understood and accepted, just as our negative feelings do. I needed to find out what my shame was trying to reveal and, more importantly, how my shadow was trying to serve me.

The gift of not being good enough, and not mattering, which came through as I wrote my book, was freedom. When I was straining to be good enough and to matter, I felt stuck because there was so much pressure to prove myself. Accepting my concern about not being good enough, and not mattering, became the most beautiful gifts, allowing me to simply share from my heart all the wisdom I have gained through Divine Grace. No longer was I trying to write a best-seller; I was simply trying to teach what I knew to whomever I could help.

The freedom you feel when you recognize the gift of your Shadow is what allows your best self to shine. No longer does your energy have to try to prove the Shadow wrong. Now all your energy can focus on your calling instead.

When you attempt to fight your ego, you are actually empowering it. You are using its language of judgment and fear. Remember, **the ego relinquishes power once you reclaim more of yours.** You reclaim more of your power by learning to honor and acknowledge the gifts of your Shadow..

Your feelings are key to awakening to the Shadow. How else do you become conscious of the ways in which your ego has its hold on you? Not knowing how to work with negative feelings has kept us trapped in the fear version of our ego's messages for too long. We can no longer waste our time being unnecessarily stuck. Your ego is a quick character, yet now you have the deeper understanding as well as the love necessary to illuminate your relationship with your ego once and for all!

OPEN YOURSELF TO FEAR

FEAR OVERWHELMS YOU WHEN IT IS ATTACHED TO YOUR EGO.
The fact of the matter is, fear is often the voice of your ego convincing you to buy into lies that do not serve you. Unaware of how your fears are trying to throw you off your path, you react, and end up self-sabotaging — one of your worst fears.

The reactive part of fear is what often does not serve you. What you are reacting to are beliefs, and the more your beliefs are attached to your ego, the more your actions are not going to serve you. You end up making your fears a reality.

Because fear can be so tricky to navigate, thanks to the cunning ways of the ego, this chapter is about breaking down fear to understand how and why it triggers you. Understanding the triggers, you can learn to choose another option. The other option is to open yourself up to your fears and recognize instead the loving guidance and energy available in fear to break through perceived limitations. In doing so, you open yourself up to more of your innate power, empowering you to more freely be you!

Through opening yourself to fear from the standpoint of love, what occurs is that fears, which once weighed on you heavily, simply no longer exist. In fact, often after working with clients, I have to remind them of how they used to get triggered. Once you can see through the eyes of love what your fear is trying to teach you, the trigger no longer works on you. You will also learn how to use the energy of fear to move you forward, rather than hold you back.

FEAR IN THE EMOTIONAL STONE AGE: THE GOOD, THE BAD, AND THE UGLY

There is goodness in how we understand fear in the Emotional Stone Age. The good and useful part of fear is how it keeps you safe by warning of potential harm. Fear, from this perspective, is what has led to your birth and survival.

Unfortunately, the larger part of fear in the emotional Stone Age doesn't serve you. Back then, it was unclear how your fear is also trying to keep your authentic self safe. Your false self was created as a place where you could hide your true self after experiencing your true self not being honored. Your fear ends up causing you pain because you remain caught within your false self for protection, even when your inner guidance is urging you to let go of some of those layers of protection. In other words, past experiences which made you feel unsafe to share your true self, now become triggers. To try to keep your true self safe, your fear pulls emotional triggers, even though you are now ready to feel the joy of sharing more of your authentic self.

What's more, fear keeps you blocked. You find it difficult to make decisions because you are bombarded with self-doubts. You keep wishing for a more fulfilling life rather than actively creating one because your energy is sapped by your fears, rather than flowing toward your inner loving guidance.

Last but not least, fear in the emotional Stone Age becomes downright ugly when you believe in your fears more than in your truth. You believe in the fear version of self (what you judge and makes you feel shame) more than you believe in your true beauty, gifts, and light. Having your energy sucked into this maelstrom of fear leads to anxiety, panic attacks, and depression (just to name a few) because you have lost connection with your essence.

UNDERSTANDING FEAR IN THE EMOTIONAL STONE AGE

In the emotional Stone Age, fear often shapes your reality. Your fear of being a failure leads you to worry and procrastinate rather than take action to realize your dreams. Your fear of rejection keeps you timid and suspicious, resulting in self-loathing. Your fear of not being liked makes you don a mask and act weirdly, resulting in few being able to know or enjoy your authentic self, and you feeling unlikable. Your fear of not getting what you want keeps you in a state of desperation, where you end up getting in your own way and blocking the flow.

Your ego convinces you that listening to your fear protects rather than hinders you (or those you love) when you follow its guidance. But what exactly is your fear protecting you from? Your fear is trying to protect you from pain. To do this, fear enlists the support of your rational mind to provide "evidence" that your fears are legitimate. Your rational mind then resurrects past experiences to create "what if" scenarios, and conjures future incidents to keep you caught in paralyzing dread.

Working as a team, your ego and your rational mind have succeeded in keeping you in darkness, and out of the present moment. Clever strategy! The conniving duo knows that the present moment is your portal to inner wisdom. And inner wisdom is your guiding light to the fullest expression of self.

Relying heavily on your fear-driven rational mind often leads to predictable outcomes. One is an analytical dead end, where you stagnate as your mind tries to figure out the "perfect/right/best solution." The result is that you never take the necessary action to create a positive shift in your life. Another outcome is taking continuous action toward whatever makes you feel safe, yet doesn't effectively serve your highest good.

For many of you, the rational mind has become a safety zone. There, you believe you can figure things out and take the necessary precautions to keep yourself away from most pain and loss. In a recent interview I did with Dr. Mollie Marti, a performance psychologist, she shared how fear is hardwired into us in a way that does not serve our highest good. She explained: "We seek comfort and instant gratification. We pull back from risk and fear, which limits (us). Your subconscious keeps you safe and secure, which can be working against everything you want."

Your fear says, "Follow my way and I'll keep you safe." Your job as a consciously evolving human is to determine what exactly you are keeping yourself safe from. Are you in danger of losing your life, or is the danger actually the loss of your false self? Fear does not discriminate between the different types of losses. By becoming conscious of your fears, you can learn to make the distinction.

The loss of your false self is the loss of your cover. Your false self is a refuge of safety where you learned to hide your brilliance. Yet a part of you knows that you and your gifts are meant to be exposed and shared. The result is unconscious ambivalence, which is an internal struggle between your ego's desire to keep you safe at all costs and your essence's desire to fulfill your life's work.

YOUR UNCONSCIOUS AMBIVALENCE

With every desire you have, there is an opposite dynamic longing to keep your life the same. Same equates with safety. Your rational mind knows you can already manage your current reality. The question is, can you handle all that will be required of you when you follow your inner guidance? Right now, an unconscious part of you fears that the answer is *no*. Of course, nobody wants to be seen as a "chicken," cooped up forever in a risk-free environment. This is especially so when an aspect of life isn't going that well, or a part of us longs desperately for greater fulfillment.

Because your false self cannot tolerate the unflattering notion of actually choosing not to change, your false self gives birth to fear to avoid disappointment. Now you have a tireless scapegoat, constantly providing you with reasons as to why you can't or shouldn't change. You then blame yourself for not being able to make your desired change. You aren't focused, dedicated, or (fill in the blank) enough to make your goal a reality. And just like that, your ego wins!

When fear is known only through the eyes of your ego, you struggle to create the change your heart desires because you are no longer connected to your heart. You're in your ego. The result is self-sabotage, confusion, and staying stuck in your ambivalence. Most of us let the pain of being who we currently are build until it is intolerable and we are backed against a wall and forced to change. Fortunately, by learning to consciously understand your fears, you don't have to create unnecessary pain in order to move forward on your path.

HIDDEN BEHAVIORS OF FEAR

Your clever ego tries not to make your fears obvious. Instead, they are subsumed in behaviors that don't serve your highest good. The brilliance behind this ego strategy is that you naturally blame yourself for these behavioral patterns rather than recognize your ego at work. These behaviors make you believe you aren't disciplined enough, strong enough, focused enough, etc.... rather than seeing your fear in action. When this occurs, you beat yourself up or push to try harder, rather than recognize what is really going on. Below are the three most common behaviors that signify unconscious fear is sabotaging you!

1. Avoidance: Common measures of avoidance include denial and putting a positive spin on an issue that you know needs attention. Pretending to ignore or set aside problematic situations is also avoidance. In this case, you trick yourself into believing that not making a choice is neutral rather than a choice in and of itself.
   Avoidance sounds like:
   - "I can't do X because I don't have enough _____ (time, money, patience, etc..)."
   - "I don't know what my choice is, so I will figure it out later."
   - "X isn't so bad, at least (fill in the blank with what is good)."

2. Procrastination: Rather than totally deny what you need to do, you know you have to take action, yet find reasons not to do so. Distraction and lack of prioritization are common. Common procrastination behaviors include:
   - Stopping what you are doing to check your email.
   - Doing menial tasks rather than a big project that needs your attention.
   - Taking lots of snack or water breaks.

3. Worry: With worry, your energy is tied up in the future by thinking about "what if." Being future-focused enables

you to escape the present. When you are not in the present, you are not able to connect with your inner wisdom. Instead, your energy is attached to the ego belief that you can have ultimate control over future outcomes via detailed plans and good intentions.

When you recognize the shapes and forms your fear shows up in, such as the above behaviors, you are able to make a conscious choice. The options are: Allow your ego to keep you sidetracked, or listen to what your essence urges you to do. When you see these behaviors in action, you're able to wake yourself from the sleepwalking you've been doing and instead choose consciously to serve your highest self.

UNDERSTANDING FEAR FROM A PLACE OF LOVE

Emotional consciousness shows fear as a great signal: the clash between what your ego wants you to do and the inner guidance of your essence. It also means that you are evolving. Fear expresses the tension between your ego's protection and your essence telling you you're ready to live in greater truth.

There are times when you cannot see the false beliefs associated with your fears because you are caught up in the portion of that fear that may come true. Your fears get activated because they feel very real and actually have the potential to become your reality. In the emotional Stone Age, this possibility would have triggered self-sabotage. Emotional consciousness, on the other hand, asks you to listen to how you react to the fear, regardless of how grounded in reality it may be, and consider that it may be rendering you powerless.

Mary was a perfect example of experiencing the very real fear of losing her home. Between student loans and her husband losing his job, they simply weren't earning enough to maintain the payments. She found herself receiving phone calls from the bank, threatening foreclosure. Despite her attempts to put in more hours and push her husband to find another job, nothing was working. Mary's fear led her to avoid creditors and the reality of her financial situation, while praying for a miracle to save her and her family.

When Mary and I spoke, she told me how afraid she was of losing her home. What I wanted Mary to see was that she wasn't just afraid of losing her home. Even deeper than her fear of losing her home was fear of being a failure. The thought of being a failure filled Mary with shame. Her shame made her want to do anything and everything she could to avoid experiencing failure. Unknowingly, trying to avoid her shame is what kept her from addressing her current reality from an empowered standpoint.

You see, Mary's fear wasn't supporting her in facing her reality. Her fears were pushing her to run away from reality with thoughts such as: "If I could just put in more hours each week we could make the payment." The reality was that she had tried working harder, but even with the extra money, they were still behind on other loans. Instead of facing the truth of losing her home, she was looking for an escape clause.

As Mary and I talked, I could sense her essence wanting to experience greater freedom. Her truth was that she felt trapped by her home. Too much of her income was going to her house. Although this house had been her dream, it no longer gave pleasure, due to the financial strain of living there. Her fear of failure told her that walking away from her home would make her an inadequate and undeserving loser. At the same time, essence was guiding her to redefine success according to her own standards rather than her ego's definition. As Mary reconnected to the yearning in her heart, she could see how letting go of her home would give her family the freedom to live with greater financial integrity moving forward. In other words, this "loss" would allow her to be her true version of success by living in financial integrity!

Once Mary was able to see what this challenge was expanding her to do – let go of her ego's version of success and live in greater alignment with her inner truth – her shame let go. Because she no longer had to carry the fear and shame of what losing her home meant about her as a person, she regained clarity and took positive forward actions. As Mary made changes to live in financial integrity, she was able to take action and avoid foreclosure. From these actions, Mary has used this experience to gain financial empowerment and totally shift the way she views herself in regard to money and success.

The whole point of emotional consciousness is to awaken from your customary reactions that are ego-based, and understand what is really powering your fear. When your reaction is attached to your ego, you will feel limited, powerless, and/or full of shame. You are the victim. When you understand your fear from the higher-consciousness perspective, you understand how your fear is present to serve you. In fact, sometimes fears occur in order to strengthen you at your core and remind you of who you truly are. The more you can recognize your truth, regardless of external circumstances, the more you are able to move forward in creating a truly fulfilling life.

"CLEAR YOUR FEAR" EXERCISE: CLEAR OUT THE EGO

VERSION OF FEAR TO ACCESS THE LOVING ENERGY COMING

THROUGH YOUR FEAR

I know firsthand that choosing essence over ego is easier said than done. Yet, living emotionally conscious means you are willing to sacrifice short-term comfort for long-term expansion. To assist you in choosing your essence over your fear, I've developed a ten-step process that helps you to realign with your essence. For the first few times, write out your responses. After that, you can apply the process in your head in a matter of moments!

1. Describe your fear from the standpoint of your ego.
2. What specific messages do you hear that limit or feel disempowering to you?
3. What fear might come up if you were to stand in your truth?
4. In what way/s is your fear trying to keep you in a role or habits that no longer serve you? (Examples include but are not limited to: Remaining the good girl/guy, wanting approval rather than being willing to lead, or wanting to fit in.)
5. Describe your attachment to that role or habit.
6. According to your fear, how would you feel if you acted in accordance with your higher self?
7. According to your higher self, how would you feel if you acted in accordance with your higher self?
8. Envision yourself as the person you would like to be, handling that fear.
9. What step can you take to move forward and act upon the guidance of your highest self immediately?
10. Affirm (and pray, if you like) that all outcomes will be

for the highest good of yourself and everyone involved.

COMMIT TO ADDRESSING THIS FEAR THROUGH LOVE RATHER THAN EGO, AND TRANSFORMATION IS YOURS!

Let's use an example that will show you how this process is applied to real life. Sharon hated confrontation, which is why she felt dread in the pit of her stomach every time her friend popped over her place unannounced. Her friend Carol always drank too much, was loud, and a huge gossip. Sharon, quite frankly, wasn't getting much out of their friendship any longer. Yet Carol always seemed to find her way to Sharon's place because their daughters were good friends.

1. Sharon's fear was about confronting Carol with her need for some distance in their relationship. Wanting distance felt harsh since they were neighbors. Sharon even began to chide herself, thinking maybe she should be more tolerant. After all, Carol had gone through a divorce only a year ago. Plus, Carol didn't have many others to turn to when she was feeling upset. Sharon thought: *If I were a good friend, I wouldn't turn her away in her time of need.*

2. Sharon was able to see how her ego was trying to make her feel guilty for how she felt about Carol. Her ego was telling her: *If you were a nicer person, Sharon, you wouldn't be so uptight about offering a little bit more of your time. A good person would help Carol rather than kick her to the curb.*

3. Sharon's fear was that if she spoke her truth, she wouldn't be liked or approved of by others. Friends and family would think badly of her.

4. Sharon could now see how her fear was trying to keep her

"good girl" persona intact. In order to stay liked and approved of, you must be a good girl, who bites her tongue.

5. To Sharon, being good meant being loved. Not being good meant being an unacceptable, mean, or bad person. Above all, it meant being an outcast. Because Sharon saw herself as a good person, she wanted to do what was "right," rather than listen to her inner truth.

6. Sharon's inner guidance wanted her to set boundaries with Carol. Doing so, according to her fear voice, would mean she would be rejected by all her friends. They would finally see her true colors – a mean, heartless person.

7. Sharon's inner voice of course knew that if she followed her truth, she would feel much more inner peace. Rather than stuffing down her feelings with food or alcohol, Sharon would feel good about the energy in her home. In fact, Sharon would feel freer and more generous in sharing her true self with others because she was finally being honest about her needs and desires.

8. When she closed her eyes and saw her higher self approaching Carol, Sharon saw a compassionate, loving, and strong leader. She would speak her truth with confidence and love. Sharon would send only love to Carol, while continuing to honor her own truth. In doing so, she would feel more of her worth.

9. Now it was obvious that Sharon needed to have a heart-to-heart with Carol.

10. Sharon's heart knew that creating healthier boundaries in her home was the right move. She was also able to see how her past behavior with Carol was enabling her

friend to avoid her own challenges. Sharon offered a silent prayer that whatever words came from her mouth when she talked to Carol would be for the highest good of both.

About a week later, Sharon took the plunge. The discussion with Carol was indeed rough. Carol was offended and stormed off, swearing never to bother Sharon again. A few days after their conversation, however, Carol called Sharon to apologize. Carol could see how she'd been abusing alcohol and wondered if they would still be friends if she stopped. Sharon told Carol how much she cared for her and hoped that she would get support regarding her drinking. Even so, Sharon respectfully asked for time and space, with the caveat that if Carol ever felt in need, to give Sharon a call.

Now that it has been a couple of months after their talk, Sharon describes creating a healthy boundary between her and Carol as a weight lifted. In fact, Sharon was able to drop fifteen pounds! The energetic weight she carried from being around Carol's toxic energy is now gone. Even better is that Sharon has increasingly opened herself to other women friends. These friendships truly see and honor Sharon exactly as she is.

Carol is doing better too, now that she has sought professional support. Both Carol and Sharon have shared how each seems freed up by the changes in their lives. They now enjoy mutual respect, and honor the space that has allowed each to grow by remaining friendly yet no longer closely connected.

Although following her essence felt challenging and at times awkward, Sharon is extremely grateful she listened to the needs of her essence. Being able to work through the discomfort is proof to her that she can stand in her truth, even when doing so is difficult. She also learned that creating healthy boundaries has allowed for a more mutually beneficial relationship that is more distant yet also more honoring of each other. Sharon now uses this experience as proof that addressing her fears is worth sacrificing short-term niceties for greater long-term alignment with her truth.

FEAR VS. TRUST

Throughout this chapter, we have discussed how fear is the easier choice. It is also the choice you have been conditioned to believe in more than the deep inner knowing within you. Emotional consciousness is about learning to trust yourself again — especially your feelings – so that you may reconnect with your divine wisdom.

Rather than let fear weigh you down, use it to support your conscious growth. Fear flexes the consciousness muscle that reminds you to trust in your truth. These everyday exercises and challenges lead you to tap into strength, courage, perseverance, and talents you didn't even know existed within you.

The truth of the matter is that fear is supposed to make you feel uncomfortable. You are expanding, and to do so means you have to move out of your comfort zone. When you learn to listen to your inner guidance, you know that you can trust it. And as self-trust blossoms, you recognize that whatever the outcome may be in following your heart, it will surely support your growth. You believe with all your heart that you are being guided in the long term.

Acting on the behalf of your essence rather than fear takes trust and courage. Before you take the plunge – into a cold lake, out of an airplane, or toward your next adventure in life — try to remember that the desired outcome is worth the price of fear. You have a choice: Put ego at the wheel and use the energy of fear to drive through life with your breaks on, OR use that charged energy to take a leap, let go, and accelerate.

Until now, fear has kept you from knowing that you have nothing to fear but your longing for safety. Your ego-based longings keep you trapped in a state of lack, but you are never lacking. The opposite of lack and fear is abundance and love. Love requires trust. Moving from emotional stasis to emotional consciousness is a shift away from trying to control your feelings to trusting in their innate wisdom. This, my friend, is how you gain certainty, wherein you have no doubts about who you are and what you came here to do. **Having this degree of certainty about yourself is the gift that fear offers you.**

So then, are you ready to make the leap and see what your feelings have to offer you as well? It only gets better!

PART III

FEEL EVERY EMOTION AS LOVE

F.E.E.L. SADNESS

THE GIFT OF SADNESS IS TO
BRING YOU CLARITY!

STATISTICS CLEARLY DEMONSTRATE THAT WOMEN FEEL MORE sadness than men, and struggle with depression twice as often as their male counterparts. Why is that? Well, every perspective has its theory, from hormones to role strain (work, childcare, housework, etc.) to the problematic habit of ruminating.

Lucky for us women, right? We just seem to be burdened with being overly emotional and sensitive... Or is that gifted? True, in the emotional Stone Age women (and men who tended to be more emotionally sensitive) seemed to get a raw deal. Ingrained for hundreds of years is the belief that women's internal strength is actually a weakness!

When your strength is unconsciously and consciously misunderstood and made to feel shameful, you not only lose yourself, you no longer trust yourself. Not trusting ourselves has been the real kick in the pants! Because when you don't trust the inner knowing that comes through emotions (a.k.a. your strength), it's a lot more difficult to reclaim your truth and your power. Is it any wonder then that women are more apt to lose their truest self and therefore feel sad when their God-given essence is not recognized, honored, and cherished?

Have no doubt about it, your sadness is a gift. Whether woman or man, it is present to reclaim what you have lost. Through understanding your sadness from the higher consciousness of love, you gain the clarity to know exactly what you need to do in order to make this self-reclamation happen.

UNDERSTANDING SADNESS AND GRIEF

Sadness is about loss. It is easy to lose your sense of direction. Sadness indicates losing your way from your life's path, and gives you the clarity to find it again. Newfound clarity inspires and empowers you to reclaim those missing pieces of your essential self, and the truth you have left or lost along your journey.

Before we get into sadness more deeply, I want to speak about grief. Grief is a particular kind of sadness in which you mourn the loss of someone you love. Your mourning actually enables you to anticipate and process what your life will now be like without your loved one's physical presence. A part of you is lost in the life you once had, and you are left to figure out how to live with your current reality. By allowing yourself to grieve, you allow yourself to transition from your "past life," which included the physical presence of your loved one, to finding a way to thrive without them by your side. As you allow the grief to come through your sadness (along with other emotions), greater clarity is gained about how you can live a fulfilled life, while also accepting your loss.

Although many considerations of sadness relate to grief, I am going to be speaking more specifically of the sadness brought about by losing aspects of your fullest expression of you. I believe that throughout life, more and more aspects of ourselves arise, seeking expression. There is such depth to each human soul!

Novel experiences, or those perceived in ever greater light, activate previously unexplored aspects of our authentic selves. It is for this reason that our sadness exists.

Sadness is present to support you in letting go of old aspects of self, layers of ego protection you no longer need. As explained in the ego chapter, we usually resist sharing in deeper and more meaningful ways. Expressing yourself more fully simply isn't what you know or feel comfortable with, and therefore feels threatening. Sadness, when understood from love, serves as your signal to embrace greater clarity and insight as to what more wants to be expressed.

Your sadness enables you to uncover your buried treasure, lovingly hidden behind your ego. Shorter stints of sadness give insight into relatively easy shifts you can quickly make in your life. The longer it has been buried, the grander the treasure you will find, and the deeper the sadness you will feel.

Without emotional consciousness, your ego keeps you going round and round, impelled by the ego's definition of who you are. You want the sadness to stop because there seems to be no point to it. Inevitably, your energy pours into trying to get rid of how you feel, without understanding the cause of your sadness.

A SAD STORY – HOW SADNESS WORKS WHEN NOT UNDERSTOOD THROUGH LOVE

Sadness permeated my life in my twenties, yet you never would have known there was pain within me. I was a master of disguise, portraying a confident, self-assured, happy, beautiful young woman. Internally, I felt none of those attributes belonged to the real me. In fact, I felt just the opposite: insecure, not good enough, not pretty enough, and overall that there was something very wrong with me. Which is why, of course, I worked so hard to project an image of the woman that I hoped people would see. I didn't want them to see the real me. The real me, I felt, was completely unlovable.

The problem with considering yourself not good enough is that no matter how hard you work at "bettering" yourself, you never reach a level of self-satisfaction or fulfillment. Sure, you may achieve your goals, and sometimes I would actually meet my objective. Even then, my efforts were never enough, as I would quickly discover why that goal still did not hit the mark.

Striver was a great description of me. I was constantly striving for something more: look better, achieve more, find love, have a cleaner home. The list could go on and on. Is it any wonder then that I found myself sad? I was exhausted from always trying harder and harder. My release was to drink myself silly on the weekends. Of course, I would end up doing something stupid, which would demonstrate what a bad person I truly was. Deep down, I felt like I was not good at my core, and I believed with all my being that I had to hide that "truth."

Fortunately, the pain from the sadness I felt and hid so well finally broke me open. My shell was cracking and I couldn't keep up the façade. It was during one of my clinical psychology classes when I finally realized I had no idea who I was. Finally, I could see the shell that I was living in that I called "me." Yet, it wasn't me! The scary part was, I had no idea who I was. I was lost. Through my sadness, I was found.

F.E.E.L. SADNESS TO KEEP YOURSELF ON COURSE

My sadness continues to guide me to get clear about who I am, what I want, and whether or not I am living in alignment with my highest, authentic self. Even as I have grown to live in greater alignment, my ego can still pull at me, trying to take me off course. That's what our egos do – they distort our concepts of self.

Your ego holds judgments about nearly everything, from how hard you work, to how much time you spend with your kids, to what you eat and don't eat. The list goes on and on, from the smallest of details. Although the details may be small, they strongly impact the way you live and, most importantly, determine the degree to which you feel fulfilled and at peace.

Usually, there will be one or two areas of your life that you are ready to explore and expand, or that simply are no longer in alignment with your truth and need to change. If this change is not happening, you will feel sad. This sadness is present to awaken you to what you truly need to attend to in the present moment.

My sadness was a HUGE MOTIVATOR in writing this book! In fact, I can easily say that if it weren't for my sadness, I am not certain this book would have been written. Now this doesn't mean I was sad all the time. I wasn't. What I want you to watch for is the artful craft of how your feelings, in this case sadness, can serve you. You will see why I WANT YOU TO BE SENSITIVE to your feelings so that you can pick up on their loving guidance quickly. You see, the more keenly attuned you are to your feelings, the faster you will be at getting back on track to what will bring you fulfillment.

A part of me knew that I was supposed to write this book. Yet doing so didn't seem to fit in with my plans of building my business. I had other ideas of what I wanted to do with my work.

Time after time, I would get busy with some other aspect of my work and not touch my manuscript for days.

But when too much time elapsed away from my manuscript, my sadness was there telling me I had gotten off course. My ego was always overflowing, it seemed, with really good reasons as to why I should focus my attention elsewhere. Each time I did, it never panned out as I had hoped, and there was more time away from addressing what I really needed to get done.

Let's remember, our ego's job is to lie to us as a form of protection. The lie is your test to see if you will still bite the lure to fill some sense of lack within you. Of course, I would take the bait from time to time and find myself off my path rather than continue to trust my authentic guidance. Thankfully, each time I did, my sadness would heighten.

I did this dance with my sadness a couple times. Each time I did, I always received the same guidance: "Get back to writing your book." Fortunately, I got it after the second time. I could hear the voice inside my head say, "Oh yes, I remember. I am meant to surrender my will to Divine Will." The decision came easily as I tuned into my feelings, because although my rational mind (as well as some business associates) was telling me to do the complete opposite, my sadness made it clear which route I was supposed to take. Get off course = feeling sad. Listen to my inner guidance and write = inner peace, fulfillment, and a knowingness that this is exactly what I am meant to be doing right now.

I am grateful to my sadness for its guidance when my mind would get confused as to which direction was truly for my highest good. These experiences of taking the bait and then feeling the sadness had to happen in order for me to realize that nothing was worth taking me away from my divine guidance. You will, just as I did, start to see the ways your ego tries to lure you from your path, and recognize its bait of empty promises.

Even more exciting about sadness is that it gives you the opportunity to understand the parts of yourself that need to be addressed in order for you to live more fully expressed. Deep inside, what was really going on with me was an old perception (and fear) that tied traditional "productivity" with financial outcome. Within my sadness was a deeper layer of unraveling that was waiting, supporting, and cheering me on to reunite with even more of my truth.

The absolute beauty of our sadness is that it tells us when we are ready to address another layer of our ego positions that hinder our fullest expression of self. As long as we live, we have the opportunity to consciously grow and evolve. Our emotions instigate life-changing inner transitions that create and support shifts in our outer world. Sadness is our champion emotion, supporting us to go within, listen, and trust.

HOW TO F.E.E.L. SADNESS

Sadness is your signal to come back home to the *REAL YOU!* Sadness, in particular, wants you to know that the way you are living is making you lose connection with your true and empowered self. This bears repeating: **Sadness signals that you are living against your truth in some area of your life.** The gift of sadness is for you to get clear about what your heart and empowered self really need and want.

Although many times applying the Four Steps to Conscious Emotional Mastery (page 43) will be enough for you to gain the clarity you need, there will also be times when your sadness supports you in working through a core shame theme. When this occurs, your sadness will feel extremely heavy. During those times, use the questions below to explore the specific meaning that this sadness has for you. These questions will open the way for you to more deeply understand what this part of you needs in order to feel better. Give yourself time to explore with your higher self what is behind the ego's version of your sadness so that you may find the clarity your heart desires.

1. Why are you sad?
2. Always start out with your ego. It is the voice that you are used to hearing and your ego will want to be first anyway. Allow it this time to "speak its piece" uncensored.
3. What do/did you want to be different? (This is a circumstance that you judge or long to change.)
4. What do you tell yourself as to why the circumstances weren't/aren't different? (Look for what you are telling yourself is wrong with you, or what you shame about yourself. See Chapter 4 on ego themes).
5. What is the shame theme showing about you? (See page 58 for examples)
6. What does that theme mean from the standpoint of love?
7. How can you nourish the part of yourself that needs your attention? (What can you do to make sure this part of you is acknowledged and taken care of? Often this involves creating a daily practice that engages an aspect of yourself that has previously been dismissed).

PUTTING THE STEPS INTO ACTION: WHAT F.E.E.L.ING
SADNESS IS LIKE IN REAL LIFE

Below are a couple of real-life examples that will support you in implementing F.E.E.L. when you are sad. One example will look at a less heavy intensity of sadness, for which the four steps were taken in a matter of moments, providing the necessary clarity to move forward. The other example shows when deeper questioning supported the integration and transformation of a core shame theme.

EXAMPLE #1: WAKING UP FEELING SAD

Sarah woke up one day feeling sad and she didn't know why. There were no troubling thoughts flying through her head, or even life challenges that were coming up for her. All she knew was she felt sad. Because Sarah was a student of F.E.E.L., she was able to go through the Four Steps of Conscious Emotional Mastery in her mind.

First, she asked herself what she was sad about. What came forward was that she felt overwhelmed. Between taking care of the kids, starting her own career, and her husband's demanding job, she felt like she was constantly on the go. She felt tired, and life felt too rushed and even too demanding at times.

When she asked her essence what the higher-consciousness meaning was, her essence validated that her life was indeed busy. At the same time, her essence did not want her to feel like a victim of circumstances. Essence advised, "Ask your husband to help with folding a load of laundry each day." Sarah thought, *What on earth? How could this be important? Laundry isn't that big of a deal, plus he is working so much!* Right then, essence showed her exactly how she was trying to overcompensate with household duties because her career hadn't taken off yet and she wasn't pulling in much money. Sarah's ego had her believing that since her husband provided financial support, that she must do all the work. Her essence was basically telling her "That's baloney!"

With that direct insight and guidance, Sarah's tears quickly turned to laughter. She could now easily see the ego's manipulation. She could hardly believe how easy it was to use her sadness to see her ego in action. Just understanding what her sadness was really about, and being willing to listen to it, made her feel so much lighter!

When Sarah's husband got home that evening, she told him it would really help her mornings go smoother if he was willing fold a load of laundry for her. He didn't bat an eyelash. Sarah used that time to practice meditation every morning to ensure that her spirit would inform her day. Even better, she has barely touched the dryer ever since!

EXAMPLE #2: I AM UNWORTHY

Here it was only a couple of weeks before Christmas, and Ariel had a big choice to make. Buy herself the new computer she knew she needed, or try to salvage the barely functioning model she'd had for nearly a decade. She'd been telling herself for years that she needed a new computer for her work. This year, there seemed to be no option. Her computer was facing certain death in the near future.

Although buying herself a new computer appeared to be the logical choice, Ariel just couldn't allow herself to make the purchase. Another part of her countermanded: "Ariel, you can't afford it. Period." The idea of adding more debt to her credit card made her cringe. She felt so irresponsible that her life had gotten to this point where she couldn't even afford the basics for her business to survive. She was filled with sadness and angst about whether or not to buy the computer she desperately needed but could not afford.

Ariel knew from hearing her ego tie her up in knots, that this was a deep issue that went way beyond buying a computer. Realizing this, she took time to consciously be with her sadness. She opened her journal and reflected on the F.E.E.L. questions relating to sadness.

It occurred to her that she wanted work aligned with her life purpose to support her financially. The kicker was when she asked herself why she wanted the circumstances to be different. What came spewing from her were all the reasons that her life was in financial ruins; according to her ego, it was all completely her fault. If she had worked harder, she wouldn't be having this problem. If she had made better decisions in the past, she wouldn't be facing the debt she has today. If she weren't such a dreamer, she would have kept her well-paying job. But the biggest reason was that if she were a better person, the Universe would have sent more people her way. In other words, there was no way in hell she was deserving of a new computer, let alone anything else she wanted. The evidence was stacked up against her. Ariel felt unworthy.

Now that she could recognize the shame she felt regarding feeling unworthy of anything she wanted in her life, she went back to use the Four Steps to Conscious Emotional Mastery. Using this shame theme and her understanding of sadness, Ariel granted her ego and essence each a turn to state their case regarding her unworthiness.

One side of her journal page was titled "ego," and the other side "ESSENCE." After fifteen to twenty minutes of writing, a light bulb went off in Ariel's heart, and then her head. What her essence revealed was that no matter how successful Ariel became, her ego would always discredit that level of success as not being enough to meet its standards. There was always more Ariel could be doing, more she should be aspiring to. Although there is nothing wrong with aspiration, her ego's impossible standard of worthiness meant she could never celebrate and never rest, let alone acknowledge all the work she had done.

Ariel's essence knew exactly how to integrate her shame. Through her heart she could see her ego was right. No matter how hard she worked or how much money she made, she would never be worthy enough to her ego. She started happily shouting "I am unworthy! I AM UNWORTHY!"

She excitedly wrote me the following:

"I'm not worthy" had to do with striving again. Will I EVER be worthy enough to have x, or do y or z? The answer is no, because I'll never be good enough to my ego. There will always be something else. WHICH MEANS - I can stop trying to be worthy. I can stop trying to be someone worthy of something — a computer or anything else! This means I can let go. I'm free to be me. Whoo hoo! I'll never be worthy!"

A couple of weeks later, Ariel joyfully bought herself the computer she needed and desired. She realized buying herself a computer was a form of much-needed recognition for the hard work she has already done. Most importantly, however, she realized her essence was starved for acknowledgement. Rather than wait to need something desperately, she decided to start setting aside time each week to recognize all she does to serve others as well as honor her inner being and light. The more she did, the more she felt centered in joy and peace!

Ariel has continued to listen to the internal guidance coming through her feelings and has acted upon that guidance. Although her guidance sometimes challenges her, taking the time to listen to her sadness has enabled her to claim more of her internal power. She has since written back to tell me how it feels as if a door has flown open, with abundance flowing to her more effortlessly than ever before!

CLAIM THE GIFT YOUR SADNESS OFFERS

Sadness is present to support you to unearth, and ultimately get clear about, what is really driving your actions, behaviors, and motives. Sadness is a vital signal to your well-being, whispering (and sometimes screaming) "Slow down! You don't even recognize who is at the wheel of your life." You think you are the one guiding your life, yet many times it is your pain. Notions of not being enough, not mattering, being worthless and undeserving are what really drive your unconscious mind. Therefore, you must prove you are a good enough, or that you are worth more and deserve more. Unconsciously, you are trying to fight your pain.

Every time you feel a twinge (or a heaping helping) of sadness, you have a choice to WAKE UP to its gift or follow your ego's lead. What this means is that whenever sadness arises, you are being given a GOLDEN OPPORTUNITY! You are being shown that a part of you that has been lost in your ego's stories is ready to be found, accepted, and honored! Sadness is present to let you know that NOW IS YOUR TIME to LET GO of the smallness you glom onto and instead claim more of your greatness.

- Remember, your sadness is present so that you will ask yourself: "What does my empowered self really want and need?" and live from that answer rather than from fear.

Rejoice in your sadness! The time has come to reveal more of you, your gifts, and your light!

F.E.E.L. ANGER

THE GIFT OF ANGER IS TO
RECLAIM YOUR POWER!

FROM THE STANDPOINT OF LOVE, THAT SURGE OF ENERGY YOU
feel when you get angry is there for you to claim more of your
power. You see, we become angry when we feel powerless. When
you are aligned with your inner truth, you are never powerless.
From a spiritual perspective, powerlessness is inconceivable!
Unfortunately, believing we are powerless happens all too easily
for most of us.

Remember (yet again!) that your ego believes it is keeping
you protected. It doesn't want your vulnerabilities exposed. Yet
to claim your true sense of power, you are actually being called
to be more vulnerable. Whether you are the person being treated
unfairly by another, which is causing you to be angry, or you are
the person unfairly treating another in your fit of anger, both
scenarios involve vulnerability to reclaim your power.

For example, let's say you were in a relationship in which
someone did not speak to you respectfully. Your anger would
show up in order for you to take a stand for yourself and insist
that the disrespect end. Although sticking up for yourself feels
like a powerful move, you have to first be willing to be vulnerable
to access your power. The vulnerability you must be open to

carries the risk that the relationship may end because you spoke up. Your ego tries to convince you to ignore your anger in order to "protect" you from feeling unloved, alone, or even without a job. It uses your vulnerabilities as fear to ignore your anger. In the short term, you feel temporarily safe when you choose to dismiss your anger. "Letting it go" and "rising above it all" seem to prevent all manner of unpleasantries – except that the anger never actually leaves! In the long run, your anger simply festers. Disregarding your feelings guarantees you won't be able to create the life you long to live. Instead, the anger turns inward and/or toward unsuspecting others. And all because you don't yet trust your power.

On the other hand, you could also be the one who is using anger unfairly toward another. Again, it's a matter of protecting yourself from feeling vulnerable. At the slightest threat, your ego goes into overdrive to conceal your sense of powerlessness. Most likely, you have no idea that you feel powerless. In fact, your ego is working especially hard to protect you by making you think you are powerful when you use physical strength, harsh actions, or sharp words against another. The result is a short-term fix that allows you to temporarily cover up the powerlessness you feel. The long-term impact when reacting from the ego's anger is a greater sense of disempowerment and dis-ease.

You feel disempowered because using the ego's brand of anger is only going to make you feel like an ass. (The nicer way of saying this is that you were completely out of alignment with your higher truth, but none of us say that to ourselves when we act out of ego's version of anger.) Being an ass means you either get caught up in trying to compensate for your out-of-control behavior or berate yourself for being such a jerk. Neither of these outcomes supports your claim to more of your power, which is why you remain in fear.

Fortressed in fear, you don't know what to do differently when similar circumstances arise. While you may swear with all your heart that you'll react to your anger differently, you struggle because deep down you feel powerless. This unconscious sense of powerlessness is what keeps you caught in reactivity, rather than being able to make a choice that serves your highest good and the highest good of others.

To make matters worse, the more powerless you feel, the more quickly you are going to find yourself caught in anger's vicious cycle. You lash out and then you compensate/berate until something sets you off again. And the more you try to compensate and/or berate yourself, the easier it will be for your anger to get set off again. That's because you're sure you are "trying your best." **What you are unconsciously trying your best at is protecting your vulnerability, which only makes you feel weaker.** In order to break the cycle of anger, you must consciously choose to wake up to what your anger is telling you: take responsibility for your own sense of powerlessness!

PARADIGM SHIFT: ANGER — THE DEADLY EMOTION?

Have no doubt about it, anger can be destructive. You've seen that destruction yourself in countries at war, relationships broken, and business partnerships ended, all because of unexamined anger. Science is even demonstrating how anger negatively impacts our health, with some even calling it the "deadly emotion." The relationship between anger, heart attacks, and other physical ills is well documented.

Given the evidence against anger, the focus has turned to trying to defuse its energy. Some methods of dissipating anger are through steps to help "talk you down," while others try to ignore anger, attempting to instill compassion instead.

Here's the problem: we need anger! It's obvious that anger can be destructive. But sometimes destruction is needed and necessary to clear away the old and make way for the new. The key is intention.

Anger came through even "The Prince of Peace," Jesus, in order to wake people up from the selfish way they treated one another. It was anger that led Dr. Martin Luther King to take a stand for civil liberties. And, it was anger, coupled with grief and sadness, that fueled mothers who lost their children to drunk drivers to create M.A.D.D. Through anger, old ways of being that did not serve the highest good were deconstructed. The result was positive transformation.

Positive transformation doesn't happen if try to put a smiley face over your anger or sweep it under the rug. Where would we be without the anger, and therefore the message, that came through Jesus, the Reverend Dr. Martin Luther King Jr. and M.A.D.D.? What we have experienced through their anger is the transformative power when anger is used from a place of love rather than fear.

Rather than try to defuse or transform anger into something it isn't (like compassion), let's instead try to understand what makes this feeling arise. When most people describe to me what happens when they get angry, they simply say "something set me off." Often the reasons are accompanied by the blaming of another person, or attributed to "bad luck" circumstances. In other words, something happened that felt out of their control and they didn't know how to handle it. Through the limited view of their ego and rational mind, there was no solution available.

Do you think the rational mind or ego of Dr. Martin Luther King Jr. was telling him that he, an African American living in the United States in the 1960s, could spearhead a movement that would bring greater equality to a country that considered him a second-class citizen? Do you think the rational mind of Candy Lightner, the founder of M.A.D.D., was telling her that her efforts would save thousands of lives? No way! Yet what propelled these people was not their rational mind. What propelled them was their essence coming through their passion that was awakened by their anger. Their essence was calling for a deeper transformation, which is how they used their anger to energize their efforts.

When anger's message is blame, you want revenge or to inflict pain onto another. This is the ego's version of anger. When anger's message is change, you deeply desire to effect transformation for the greater good of all involved. With love energizing your anger, you ignite passion, which is contagious! This is true of countries, groups, and individuals. Anger isn't the problem. The problem is the lens through which anger is seen and acted upon.

When you see an individual, group, or country expressing anger from ego, all feel disempowered. Unfortunately, most don't realize that the ego version of anger actually reinforces the current circumstances so that they remain the same. Fighting a sense of disempowerment by disempowering another only generates more fear. From fear, no one can feel empowered to create lasting change. What is left is more anger that continues to build until it explodes, with dire consequences – or simmers ("does a slow burn"), until a higher consciousness heeds the call for change.

We need to end the evil spin that has been put on anger. From love, anger is present for you to recognize more of your internal power. Your anger is present to let you know when your boundaries are being violated, or when circumstances are not for the highest good of all. It is there to support you as you bring about the conscious change that is needed in your life and in the world.

AN ANGRY STORY

Mary wore her anger like a badge of honor. In fact, she took pride in her tough-girl persona. The problem was, when you live your life using anger as your protection, it's difficult to find happiness. Mary didn't realize she was using anger as a form of protection; she only knew she felt unsatisfied with the way life was turning out for her.

Mary's anger was actually an old habit she learned when she was very young. When we are young, we of course try to meet our parents' standards and expectations. Many of us end up in adulthood like Stuart Smalley, still trying to be "good enough" to meet those standards. That leads us down a path of straining to be nice, liked, and accepted. If this is the case for you, then you likely feel hesitant to express your anger because of your fear of disapproval.

Mary, however, felt there was nothing she could get right. In order to spiritually survive feeling rejected right down to her core, she had to give up trying to please her parents. Her only defense against sadness at being deeply rejected was to get angry.

Most people are unaware that they can't feel anger unless they first feel sadness. Anger masks sadness so that we don't feel so vulnerable. It offers a false sense of getting needs met through a show of power, when deep down one feels powerless.

Mary felt powerless to ever receive the acceptance and love she needed. Her anger, however, allowed her to become the one who now did the rejecting. Through that anger, she could reject her own need for love and acceptance, as well as the potential for painful disappointment inherent in any act of love sent her way.

Mary's anger allowed her to assume the identity of a person who was completely independent, tough, smart, and most importantly, one who didn't need anyone. Anger was her armor against her biggest vulnerability, being rejected by others first. The toughness she projected kept others at a safe distance.

The problem was that Mary's defensiveness, which came off to many as offensiveness, limited her ability to express herself authentically. Even though Mary's ego had her believe she was being totally herself because she could act as mean, bold, or scary as she liked, Mary still wasn't living authentically. Beneath that tough exterior was her potential for love, kindness, joy, and compassion. You see, Mary really was a kind soul, yet no one but her animals was allowed to get close enough to experience that goodness. Her animals were safe, never rejecting her; humans, on the other hand, could reject her just as her parents had.

By enacting this angry role, Mary was hiding from her real gifts. Her anger kept her safe yet unfulfilled. Unknowingly, Mary was now rejecting herself, just as she was rejected as a child. Even though she easily expressed her anger, her *real* anger was directed inward, making her powerless to create the life she truly desired to live.

F.E.E.L. ANGER TO KEEP YOU ON COURSE

When anger isn't used for its higher purpose, which is to

claim one's true sense of power, it turns inward. Even though Mary felt like she was a powerful woman because she easily expressed her anger, she wasn't claiming her true power. As a result, she felt deep-rooted anger toward herself because she was unwilling to step into her true strength.

You don't have to be an outwardly angry person to have anger festering inside of you, either. During a time in my life when I was feeling disappointment, I sought out the support of a few different spiritual advisers. Each of them gave me the same message: "Michelle, you are angry!" I didn't *feel* angry, so at first I blew off the message. Yet, after a second and third mention of my anger, I knew I had to dig deeper.

What I came to realize was that beneath my disappointment was, in fact, anger. At the time, I was working my butt off without getting many results. Deep down, I felt there was nothing I could do that would change the situation, besides change careers. Aha! There was my sense of powerlessness! I felt powerless about my work. Unconsciously, I was swallowing my anger, as my ego cleverly disguised it as disappointment!

Once able to recognize my anger, I could now acknowledge that I **did indeed** have power over my circumstances. By recognizing the anger in my disappointment, I was able to see that I did have a choice (and choice gives us power). My choice had to do with how I went about my work. Even though I thought I worked in a balanced way (for instance, going to yoga once a week and getting a massage once a month), I also carried a deeply held belief that was working against how I approached my work. That belief was: If you work hard, you will produce the results you want. With that belief glued to my ego, my rational mind assumed I wasn't getting the results I desired because I wasn't working hard enough. The problem was that no matter how hard or long I worked, the results didn't change.

The anger festering within me was from my Inner Wise Self, and was she ever pissed! She wanted time to play. Realizing I must still be imbalanced, I tried making my essence a priority each morning. Yet, the time I gave never felt enough to this part of me. Then I became angry at this aspect of myself. And to this playful, no-cares-in-the-world side of me I snapped: "What more do you want? I have kids to raise and important work to do. I can't spend my life playing all the time!" It felt like this part of me was being a demanding brat. She thought I (the part of me being run by my ego) was being a bitch.

Now believe me, I know it sounds weird to get angry at parts of my own self. Yet most of us do it all the time. We have parts of ourselves pulling us one way and other parts pulling us another. The only difference is that emotional consciousness allows us to identify who is pulling and why, so we can understand the underlying gift.

What my anger helped me realize was that my ego had no time for play. According to my ego, play was earned and I hadn't earned that privilege yet. No wonder my Essence was angry! Because my self-worth was tied to results, my ego expected my sacred, playful Inner Wise Self to show up day in and day out to create magic in my life. And here I thought I was showing my Sacred Self love and affection by getting my monthly massage, or taking a long bath every so often. To Her, that was like throwing the dog a bone and saying, "There you go, pal! That should take care of you for a while. Now let me get back to more important matters." What I wasn't doing was acknowledging Her as my fuel, my creative fire, the light that She was and continues to be. As in any nourishing relationship, She didn't want things; she just wanted to be acknowledged for her part. She didn't need more time devoted to her, per se. What this part of me needed was to be fully seen for the gift She brought me, and honored for it.

The higher consciousness of my anger was present to teach me to heal another layer of my self-worth. I wanted external acknowledgment. Yet, the Universe could not reflect back to me what I did not feel worthy of giving myself. In order to receive acknowledgment, I first had to learn to embrace self-acknowledgment at a deeper level. When I did not feel worthy of the degree of acknowledgment that my Inner Wise Self desired, I was also communicating not feeling worthy of external acknowledgment. My anger was guiding me to finally acknowledge myself at the depth my heart desired so that I could open my external experiences to even more fulfillment.

Through recognizing the needs beneath my anger, I was able to utilize this once misunderstood and harshly judged part of me, and integrate my essence more fully into my work. Now, rather than feeling pulled by one side or the other, I am learning a deeper sense of inner balance. With this balance comes focus, and a much freer flow of creativity.

As inner balance deepened, I felt increasingly empowered, not only in my work, but also in how I went about my life. Only through emotional consciousness will your anger teach you how to love yourself more deeply. Thanks to my anger, I learned to reclaim a deeper sense of power, which continues to support me to stay on my life's course with greater effectiveness, joy, and grace!

HOW TO F.E.E.L. ANGER

By now you probably realize that simply releasing your anger, or any of your feelings for that matter, is not the same as F.E.E.L.ing. The key to F.E.E.L.ing is to understand the message within each emotion so that you will take action in alignment with love. Absent this understanding, the feeling just continues to come back. This is why whenever energy or spiritual workers would try to clear my anger, the feeling would ultimately return. I wasn't getting to the core of what my anger meant. More importantly, my anger was coming through to support me to make conscious changes in the way I related to my work. **The bottom line is that regardless of how many times or ways you try to release an emotion, the feeling will return when the higher guidance hasn't been acted upon.**

To act upon the loving guidance of your anger, first remember that it is a gift: a fierce wind to blow the lid off boxed-in essence, wherein lies your authentic power! In other words, whatever is causing you to feel angry is because you haven't fully claimed your true sense of power. Anger is signaling to you that YOU are taking away your own power by how you perceive the situation.

To understand the meaning that's specific to your anger, utilize the Four Steps to Emotional Consciousness (page 43). Below are some deeper questions regarding anger to assist you in further recognizing the core message behind your anger's sense of powerlessness:

1. What triggered your anger? (i.e., someone not listening to you, feeling disrespected).
2. What did you take that person's reaction or the situation to mean about you? (i.e., I feel disrespected and not

honored for how I feel).

3. What area of your life (besides the current circumstance seeming to cause your anger) would you want to be different?

4. Why haven't you been able to change that area of your life? (Keep the focus on yourself, rather than blaming another or your circumstances.)

5. In what ways do you judge/treat yourself similarly to how you believe others are treating you? (Look at your response to question #2 and see the connection between what you take circumstances to mean about yourself and your judgment of yourself.)

6. How are you being guided to change how you treat yourself?

PUTTING THE STEPS INTO ACTION: WHAT F.E.E.L.ING ANGER IS LIKE IN REAL LIFE

Below are a couple of real-life examples to help you implement F.E.E.L. when it comes to your anger. The first example used only the Four Steps to Conscious Emotional mastery and was done within a matter of minutes. The second example demonstrates how to get to the core message, even when you may feel resistant, by addressing the questions above to support deeper recognition and healing of a core shame theme.

EXAMPLE #1: I'VE BEEN DEALT A BAD HAND

During one of my group coaching calls, Amanda hopped on the line to share her lifelong struggle with anger. Although she considered herself a very spiritual person who tried to be good and to serve others as best she could, she felt she had been dealt a bad hand. Her father left her and her mom when she was only a baby. He left after realizing that Amanda was born with a paralyzing birth defect that would leave her with physical challenges for the rest of her life. Amanda and her mother turned to their faith as they went through numerous trials and tribulations throughout the years.

She said to me, "Michelle, I know anger is about reclaiming my power, but I haven't been able to find any. I really do feel like I am a victim. I don't feel helpless, but I do feel that I don't have any control over the circumstances I've been dealt."

I understood. Her circumstances had caused her a great deal of pain on all levels, physically, mentally, emotionally, and spiritually. The truth is that Amanda, as well as anyone else who feels like a victim, is justified in feeling that way.

I agreed with Amanda that her life was riddled with circumstances that caused her pain since she was born. I also validated that her circumstances would cause just about anyone to feel like a victim. What I challenged Amanda with was her choice in perspective as to how her circumstances were being used to define herself. "How situations define you is always a choice, and that is where your power is," I reminded her.

I then quickly reminded her of the life of Nelson Mandela. Mandela had the choice to view his imprisonment from the standpoint of the victim or from a place of higher consciousness. He had every right to choose to view his situation as a victim. How he was treated was unjust. Yet, Mandela chose to express strength, courage, endurance, and personal power. He did this by surrendering to his reality and allowing his circumstances to further impassion him. In doing so, he was still able to impact the future of his country, even while behind bars.

Amanda suddenly got it. She could see all the ego stories bubbling up in her mind, along with much past regurgitation of same. I reminded her of "victim consciousness" as well. As the victim, you are certain to remain powerless because your focus is on lack and the wrongdoings that have been your lot. I didn't have to say any more.

Amanda interrupted, saying, "Yes, by being the victim, I am ensuring that NOTHING CHANGES. For over forty years I've been carrying this anger, and I finally see what it has wanted me to know right along!" Her essence was guiding her to take back her power by stopping her from seeing herself as a crippled child. That crippled-child image she'd held on to made her feel unlovable and unworthy.

The first action she knew she needed to take was to honor all that her physical body offered her throughout the years, rather than focusing only on the challenges. She was thrilled to finally take in on an emotional level how blessed she truly is for the life she's been given, one that has led her to grow and evolve in remarkable ways. More importantly, she committed to acknowledging herself daily for triumphs she had made throughout the years, yet had dismissed or discounted their importance.

With the insight of her essence, Amanda felt empowered to live her life from the present as a wise, intuitive woman, rather than a helpless little girl. Instead of seeing herself as helpless, she could clearly see her strength for being able to thrive under such challenging circumstances. Now she uses her little girl to cheer her on when she feels most afraid to claim more of her power!

EXAMPLE #2: WHEN RAGE IMPACTS YOUR SPOUSE

Dave and Sheila had been married for over ten years when they came to me for support with their marriage. They were distraught because it was not working, and Sheila was considering divorcing Dave. She loved Dave but was afraid of his anger and the impact it was having on their daughters. When Dave's anger escalated, he would become verbally abusive and physically confrontational. Obviously, this was not the kind of family life Sheila wanted for herself or her young daughters.

The problem was that Dave blamed his anger on Sheila. Dave, a talented energy healer, believed the core of the problem was that Sheila wasn't spiritual enough. "She's too uptight and anxious. If only she were more laid-back and relaxed, she could accept me for who I am rather than always being so nitpicky toward me and needing to get her way all the time!"

To help Dave to more deeply understand his anger, I asked him what triggered it (Question #1). He said that most of the time, his life is run by his wife. He feels that all decisions are made by her, and whatever she says goes, because she is the breadwinner of the family.

(Question #2) What do you take this to mean about you? To Dave, the way decisions were made in his relationship made him feel like his decisions were wrong or somehow not good enough to her. Ultimately, he believed his feelings didn't matter to her.

I probed further, asking (Question #3): What area of your life would you want to be going differently? Dave admitted that although he felt extremely gifted as a spiritual healer, he was not earning enough to sustain his family. Ultimately, he would like to follow his dream as an energy healer and have his work provide financially for his family.

(Question #4) Why haven't you been able to change that area of your life? Without being able to blame his wife or their current circumstances, Dave had to face the nagging voice within him. Although he tried adamantly to ignore this inner nagging because he believed in the power of positive thinking, the thought was still within him. He didn't believe that he could become successful because no matter how hard he tried, his circumstances didn't change. Even though he knew he was gifted in his work, another part of him felt powerless to bring this gift to its fullest expression — making a living in service and joy.

(Question #5) In what ways do you judge/treat yourself similarly to how you believe others are treating you? Deep within, Dave felt impotent (and also struggled with physical impotence). This made him feel weak and incapable. All the while, he tried desperately to cover up this pain with a positive, spiritual outlook. However, any time a sense of powerlessness was triggered, he would become enraged. He could finally see how his anger wasn't about Sheila. It was painful feelings of inadequacy that he was trying to ignore.

(Question #6) How are you being guided to change how you treat yourself?

Dave's anger was actually trying to guide him to take more responsibility in everyday life. He was fighting responsibility because of old notions of what responsibility meant. These old notions made him feel that responsibility was always onerously heavy, and would weigh him down. Quite honestly, he also found some of his daily tasks to be beneath him. He was a healer, not a caretaker.

What Dave didn't realize was that in judging and degrading his role as caretaker, he had unconsciously made himself a victim of circumstance. And the more he fought his current circumstances, the more his situation stayed the same. By resisting the reality of his situation, Dave was rarely wholly present with his family, and largely resentful of the duties that came with being the caretaker. His discontentment caused a huge disconnect between him and his wife, as well as his daughters.

Dave's essence made him aware that his anger was directed at himself — how he judged his role as caretaker. He was then able to connect the dots to see how he couldn't claim his power as caretaker if he was unwilling to honor that role. By not honoring his role, he was really dishonoring himself.

Begrudging his role, Dave knew he wasn't giving his best energy to his family. He'd feared surrendering to the role of caretaker, because he thought doing so would minimize his healing work. His energy work made him feel special. Without that, he felt as if he didn't matter. In other words, his ego was using his energy work to define him. Finally, Dave was able to see that by demeaning his role as caretaker, he actually took away from his sense of self.

His essence was guiding him to reclaim his power as a caregiver, by honoring rather than devaluing his role. In doing so, Dave was able to see that the resentment he bore toward his wife for being a powerful provider was really his own resentment toward himself for constantly discounting his role. Dave realized he had a choice, to either remain defined by his ego's need for self-importance or to let go and recognize the value of the lessons offered in everyday life. In letting go, Dave was free to be the person, healer, and caretaker he was meant to be! Having that true sense of inner freedom felt powerful too!

CLAIM YOUR GIFT OF ANGER

Your anger is your internal fuel, providing the impetus to take responsibility for your life. Your essence will always use anger to awaken you to greater power and a fuller, more vibrant life. Whether you have given your power away because of what someone may think of you, or you have obscured your own power by believing you are a victim, you anger will come through to speak to YOU! Anger's statement is never about anyone else and is always to remind you of this: **you have more power than you realize.**

Anger is about reclaiming your power to validate, give recognition to, and truly honor more of the truth of who you are. Allow the fire of anger to ignite within you through love rather than fear. As you do, you empower your passion to create the transformations your heart longs for.

- Remember, the gift of your anger is to help you remember your power by asking your empowered self: "How am I meant to claim my power in this situation?" and acting upon the answer you receive from love rather than fear.

The gift of anger is waiting for each of us to tap into its love and be used to serve the world! Yet, in order to do so, you must first get comfortable with claiming the gift of anger within you. Allow the energy within your anger to ignite your passion to serve with love and light, and watch with amazement the impact of your efforts on your life and world!

F.E.E.L. ANXIETY

THE GIFT OF ANXIETY IS TO DEEPEN YOUR TRUST IN YOUR HEART'S WISDOM!

ANXIETY IS PURE ENERGY WAITING FOR YOU TO USE IN SER- vice of your highest good. Anxiety amps you up and makes you want to take the leap into the unknown. Your anxiety is the energy behind bold moves that comes with trusting in yourself. This is only, of course, when you understand your anxiety through love rather than fear.

I am not the only one who holds this belief, either. Well-known actors have shared how each time prior to going on stage before a live audience, they vomit! The buildup of energy they are feeling makes them throw up each and every time. Do they curse their anxiety? They may have at first when they didn't understand why they were feeling stage fright. But after going through the experience time and again and realizing how pumped their performance was, they have learned to honor their anxiety. They learned to recognize that the power-filled energy making them upchuck is the same energy charging them up enough to create amazing performances!

When your anxiety is viewed from the higher consciousness of love, it helps you to tap into energy that calls you to be bold, brave, and courageous! Your anxiety wants you to take a leap of faith — for yourself. You remember the life your heart says it wants to have, right? The life with a certain kind of relationship, lifestyle, job, sense of self, etc., that feels fulfilling to you? Well, your anxiety shows up exactly so that you will take actions that lead you to your heart's desires.

To bridge the gap between your current reality and your heart's desire, you need to be willing to take the proverbial leap of faith. Leaping, especially the forward-life-movement kind, takes TRUST and FAITH. Unfortunately, trust and faith are what many people are short on nowadays. If we take a moment to reflect on the meaning of both words, we can begin to sense what's missing in their absence.

Definition of Trust: a: assured reliance on the character, ability, strength, or truth of someone or something **b:** one in which confidence is placed

Definition of Faith: a: firm belief in something for which there is no proof **b:** complete trust **c:** something that is believed, especially with strong conviction

There it is! In order to have trust and faith, you need to have **personal conviction.** Personal conviction means that you trust and believe in yourself thoroughly. This means you have confidence in yourself, even when there is no proof you should. Is it any wonder then that so many struggle with anxiety?

It is so darn easy to lose your sense of conviction. Conviction is lost when you lose your true sense of self, whether by people-pleasing or trying to conform to your own idea of a good person. (Something we've all done at one time or another.) You also lose your conviction when you don't have a strong allegiance to your essence because you are attached to your personality. (Easily lost when exposing your true self makes you feel too vulnerable, or if you care too much about what others think of you.) Last but not least, conviction in regard to self is lost when you don't believe with all your heart and mind that following the inner wisdom of your essence will ultimately be for your highest good. Think about how easy it is to lose conviction when the immediate results do not appear in alignment with your heart's desires.

Here's the deal. I know it isn't easy to have confidence in yourself, especially when you don't feel supported. Yet, deep within your heart, you know you are being called to believe in yourself. When you are lucky, you have people behind you, encouraging your self-confidence to grow. However, when it comes to your internal growth, where you claim more of your truth and inner radiance, it's typically a solo job. Even if you hire a coach, which I highly recommend you do to make important life changes, your coach won't physically be there by your side in each moment you are called to act on behalf of your heart. You must do that part alone. In those moments, you confront your anxiety, which is trying to keep you wrapped in fear, self-doubt, and worry. Yet when you understand your anxiety from love, you see it showing up to give you a little extra kick in the pants. What it is saying is, *"Believe in yourself!"*

PARADIGM SHIFT: FINDING PEACE THROUGH YOUR ANXIETY

When you feel anxious, your mind is racing at 100 mph. You feel pushed and pulled every which way. Plus, no matter what choice you make, you feel uncertain, leaving yourself to second-guess your every move. Sound peaceful? I don't think so!

According a 2011 study by the National Institute of Mental Health, anxiety impacts approximately 56 million Americans every year, causing some form of debilitation. For some, the anxiety is so severe that they cannot get out of bed to go to work. For others, the doubts and worries act more subtly as their "free-floating anxiety" zaps their vital energy, leaving them feeling exhausted. Regardless of how little anxiety you have, when it is attached to fear, it is guaranteed to keep you at some remove from your true self.

You see, when anxiety is heard only from your ego and rational mind, you are receiving the run-around. **You absolutely cannot think your way out of anxiety.** Yet, that is exactly what your mind has you try to do. You think of every possibility that could happen. You worry about the worst-case scenario. All of which keeps you constantly spinning.

From the standpoint of love, you recognize how anxiety is a calling of your heart. It is signaling to you that you are allowing your fear to take the lead, and it is time to give it back to your heart. Unconsciously, you fight your heart with worry and trying to control outcomes, rather than listening to its guidance.

Your ego wants you to believe in the illusion of control because if offers a false sense of safety. What really happens when you engage your ego in worry and control is you ignore the guidance of your heart. Your heart is warning you not to dismiss your inner guidance, and risk remaining unfulfilled.

Anxiety is the unconscious tug-of-war between your ego/rational mind/fear/control and heart/essence/trust/faith. Remain unconscious, and guess who's in control? You guessed it — your ego and rational mind are in the driver's seat. By becoming aware of what your anxiety is signaling to you, you gain a new choice to check into your heart.

For your heart's desires to become your reality, you must be willing to take forward action stemming from your heart. Your anxiety is simply a symptom of the fact that you are buying into fear more than love, and a friendly reminder that you may choose the path of self-love instead. Not surprisingly, when you allow your heart to take the lead, you are brought back to a state of calm and inner peace. You see, anxiety's job is to bring you back to peace by getting you to take action toward creating a fulfilling life. Then, anxiety's job is done and you naturally go back to a state of peace.

AN ANXIOUS STORY – WHEN ANXIETY ISN'T UNDERSTOOD THROUGH LOVE

If you were to look at Lucinda's life on paper, there wouldn't be much that seemed wrong. She was a top executive at a Fortune 500 company, where she was well respected. Lucinda also was married and had two beautiful daughters. She even finagled numerous weeks off to take trips back home to see her family in Denmark. As Lucinda put it, "Great job, great money, great health, and great children – I have nothing to complain about in my life." The problem was, Lucinda was not happy.

Although she was amazing at her job, Lucinda was thoroughly bored by it. She wanted to do something that truly mattered. Yet, as the financial provider for her family, she felt she had no choice but to stay in her job.

Unfortunately, life at home was even worse than her job. Her marriage was hanging on by a thread. Her husband would tell her, "If only you were more (fill in the blank) or did (fill in the blank), our relationship would be better. Even though Lucinda would try to stick up for herself, deep down she believed her husband was right.

You see, Lucinda believed she was as internally flawed as they come, making her nearly impossible to love. Trying to prove otherwise, she would push herself to take on more and more, from pole dancing (to be more interesting to her husband) to more child- care duties (even though she already took the "evening shift" after working all day). Not surprisingly, taking on more to please her husband never ended up helping her marriage. All it did was turn her daily anxiety into full-blown panic attacks.

The panic Lucinda was feeling was due to two fears. First was a fear she would die alone. Second was a fear she would never truly make a difference with her life. What Lucinda didn't realize was that by listening to her ego, she was on her way to making her fears her reality. Her ego (and her husband, for that matter) constantly told her there was more she should do. All this doing kept Lucinda away from actually being. The more disconnected she became from her authentic self, the more her life reflected her fear rather than her ideal.

Without a connection to her inner wisdom, there was no way she would ever know what kind of work would bring her fulfillment. The saying "find your passion" isn't true. Your passion finds you, and the only way it can come through is when you are open and connected enough to your essence to be able to hear its whispers.

Lucinda would never be able to have a relationship that served both herself and her partner without listening to her authentic self. Yet, she was too scared to listen to her authentic self. Her authentic self shared with Lucinda her true needs. Following the guidance of her inner wisdom, she feared, would cripple her relationship all the more. The truth was, the real Lucinda wasn't present in her marriage, which of course guaranteed that she would never have the intimate connection she desired.

Lucinda's anxiety was trying to wake her up from this horrible nightmare created by ignoring her essence. Her anxiety was saying, "Lucinda, you can no longer ignore these areas of your life and pretend that things will work out as you want. You need to take action NOW on behalf of your true self!"

To listen to her inner wisdom and make the changes she was being called to make, Lucinda needed to trust in herself. Lucinda's main problem was that she no longer had faith in herself. Her faith had been lost a few years back when her sister tragically died in a skiing accident. Lucinda was there when it happened. Although she was able to get help right away, the degree of injury was too significant. Intellectually, Lucinda realizes there was nothing more she could have done. But the nagging of her ego won't leave her alone, with "if only's" making her at fault for her sister's death.

Ultimately what Lucinda found was that her anxiety was present to support her in healing from the pain of losing her sister. Her anxiety was nudging her to reclaim trust in herself. The key, Lucinda realized, was listening to and acting upon her anxiety's loving guidance, rather than the fear coming from her ego. Seeing how fear controlled so many different areas of her life, Lucinda could now understand her choice. Her first choice had been to keep life the same by continuing to live in fear, which felt safe and comforting, even though far from ideal. Her other option was to take a risk on behalf of her essence, which felt scary but was the only true path to a fulfilling life. What she knew without a doubt was that her anxiety was going to hang around until she was willing to choose the latter.

F.E.E.L. ANXIETY TO KEEP YOU ON COURSE

The underlying cause of your anxiety is that unconsciously, you are trying to have your needs met by someone or something outside of yourself. This means that having your needs met is now beyond your control because it is based on some external component or person (spouse, child, parent, boss, money, job, friend, etc.). Your sense of control is painfully compromised because you have given the responsibility of meeting your needs to someone/thing else besides yourself. This is what makes your mind start spinning – you want to regain control to create a more fulfilled life.

Of course, you don't feel that it was you who took away your power. You feel as if you have no choice (hint: that is always a lie). Again unconsciously, you turn to acts that don't serve you to try to find relief and get your needs met, such as manipulating or self-sabotaging behaviors that give you instant gratification (i.e., eating, gossiping, shopping, checking your email). Most of these behaviors in and of themselves aren't bad. The problem is how you use them to make you feel you are okay in the short term to avoid your truth.

You renounce your truth because you feel that listening to it will mean your needs will not get met. OFTENTIMES YOU ARE RIGHT – FOR THE TIME BEING. That is, if you typically keep your mouth shut in your relationship in order to ensure your spouse's approval, and then suddenly you start sharing your opinion, your spouse is probably not going to welcome your new outspokenness. The approval you are craving won't be there, further denying the validation you seek from him/her.

With anxiety, you hear the messages of your authentic self, yet unconsciously or consciously you choose not to take actions on its behalf. Following your essence feels too scary, or totally contrary to what you actually want to accomplish. Those of you for whom approval was hard to come by when you were growing up actually became very much sensitized to what other people want. You developed a special radar, which accurately detects what will bring you approval and disapproval. This radar is always ON, leading you to be overly concerned of what people think of you and trying to people please. Having this conscious concern or unconscious agenda also makes you more prone to anxiety, because rather than being yourself, you have learned to misrepresent yourself to gain the approval you desire.

I used to be a huge people-pleaser, which would make me nervous and anxious just raising my hand in a group setting. I'd be worried about sounding dumb and saying "the wrong thing." But once I began to understand the loving guidance behind anxiety, I came to use its energy as a signal. The stronger the signal/anxiety was, the more I was able to recognize that what I had to share was important. When anxiety came up in this way, I affirmed that I recognized my sharing as important, which allowed my ego to calm down. My essence now has the room to move and speak within me, which allows my true self to express through my words and deeds. Afterwards, usually at least one person comes up to me and says, "You took the words right out of my mouth!"

Even though raising your hand in a group when you feel anxious seems like no big deal, it really is. Whenever you act upon the prompting of your heart when you feel anxiety — rather than on the contraction of fear — you are initiating a very important shift. You gain more self-trust by acting upon your inner wisdom. Small acts of trust like speaking out in a group encourage you to take greater and greater risks. Through each of these small moments, you will find your anxiety leading you to a place of blind faith, which ultimately emboldens you to take that huge leap toward realizing your life's purpose.

Even if you're not constantly trying to people-please, you are still going to have situations that feel uncomfortable. They will usually involve holding back sharing your whole truth because you are afraid that doing so would hurt another. Or maybe you feel you need to have a conversation with someone and you dread it because you feel you'll be the one to get hurt. In either case, anxiety flares to show you that what you need to share is too important to ignore.

Still to this day, my anxiety will kick in whenever I know I am being called to make a big move. While my heart is excited by the potential for new experience and growth, my ego wants my life to stay the same, thank you very much! Even when it came to writing this book, an endeavor I knew was for the highest good, my ego would jump in with numerous excuses as to what else I should be doing rather than writing. Fortunately, when I listened to my ego, my anxiety would raise a big stink. Then I would remember, "I can't blow this off, can I? Okay, I'll get back to writing!"

Conveniently, anxiety is a foolproof sign that a battle between ego and essence is raging within. Even more importantly, it can help you to discern which voice is which. My ego wasn't telling me to do something that didn't make any sense. In fact, what it was telling me to do made the most sense from a business perspective. Throughout, my essence doggedly called me to write, almost exclusively! This meant seeing many fewer clients, and a consequent loss of income. I have to admit that letting go and trusting in this way scared me. What I knew about anxiety, though, was that any short-term sacrifice was for the highest good in the long run. So I surrendered and trusted (mostly!). When I didn't, there would be my anxiety, again telling me, "This is too important, Michelle. You can't blow this off." Thankfully, I listened, and the anxiety would go away because I was taking the action I needed to move forward on my path.

HOW TO F.E.E.L. ANXIETY

Always think of your anxiety as an intelligent attention-seeking device. Rather than paying attention only to the ego view, ask yourself what your essence wants you to notice. Your essence is waving a big red flag that can't be ignored. Even if you find a way to temporarily distract yourself, your anxiety will reappear because the message is important. This red flag of anxiety is signaling that you are going the wrong way (in the direction of fear), and that you need to choose love instead.

Your essence will never give up on trying to get your attention. Your life and your purpose are too damn important not to continue to bug you until you are willing to pay attention and take action on your essence. The energy of your anxiety will push you off your comfy spot on the sofa (metaphorically speaking) and "get your hands dirty" by taking a risk on behalf of your higher self.

Again, utilize the Four Steps to Emotional Consciousness

(page 43) to address occasional anxiety. For lingering anxiety, ask yourself the questions below to understand the specific message your anxiety wants you to address and act upon.

1. What triggered your anxiety? (Look for what you fear people will see in you that you don't want them to know about the "real" you.)
2. If people saw what you were trying to hide in question #1, how would you feel?
3. What does that scared part of you need from you in the moment?
4. What shame theme is this part of you and your anxiety trying to heal?
5. How does your essence want you to take action to support this healing?

EXAMPLE #1: CONFRONTATIONS AND THE AFTERMATH

Not too long ago, Laura found herself in a predicament. Through a series of synchronistic events, she had found out that her cousin Gina had cheated on her husband years ago. Laura said, "I was really torn. There was a part of me that did not want to touch Gina's cheating with a ten-foot pole! At the same time, I felt this issue needed to be addressed, for Gina's sake." Laura confided, "With all my heart, I did not want to cause a rift. I thought I should just leave well enough alone."

Fortunately, Laura remembered from a class I taught that whenever we are torn between following our heart/essence versus our ego/rational mind, anxiety is present to help us choose our hearts. Even though she was inclined to stay out of her cousin's marital issues, she decided to go through the Four Steps to Emotional Consciousness just to be sure what part of her was guiding her choice.

She allowed her ego to share its side as to why she was anxious. Laura's ego said, "Who are you to get into their business? You should just leave things the way they are. You don't want anyone to get hurt."

Now it was her essence's turn. What she heard surprised her. "Laura, Gina is too afraid and ashamed to address her affair on her own. She is unconsciously carrying this pain and you can help her face it. Go see her in person and help her begin to resolve this affair."

Hearing the guidance of her essence, Laura's ego butted in and retorted, "You know Gina is just going to get defensive and blame you for causing trouble. She may even cut her family's communication off from yours. Is that what you want? Plus, how are you going to see her in person when she lives one hundred miles away?" Laura's head started to spin with fear and worry.

She took a breath and sunk down deep within to reconnect with her heart. Her essence told her that not sharing what she knew with Gina would keep her energetically entangled in the affair. She was guided to trust, and bravely move forward and speak with her cousin, even if it meant being cut off from Gina's family.

Laura made a plan to talk to her cousin a day after their upcoming family reunion. The reunion was three weeks away. During that time, Laura's anxiety would pop up from time to time, wanting to take her into the future of talking to Gina. Rather than allowing her mind to take the lead in coming up with the "perfect" words to say, she reminded herself why the anxiety was coming through her. "This is too important, Laura!

You can't ignore it," the loving guidance of her anxiety would say. "I won't, I promise. Just try to make this go as smoothly as possible," Laura would say as a prayer.

Ultimately, Laura acknowledged that it was her anxiety's energy that gave her the courage to speak to Gina. Laura was loving, yet completely honest, as she shared what she knew about Gina's affair. Gina was shocked, defensive, and pissed off. She even went so far as to accuse Laura of being a marriage-wrecker. Laura left when she saw the conversation was going nowhere, as she had a long drive back to her family.

As soon as Laura got into the car, her anxiety returned. She did not like leaving everything unsettled between her and Gina. She saw her anxiety trying to suggest that Gina might be right. Am I really a home-wrecker? Was I over the top in how I approached Gina? Was I too judgmental? In that moment, as she heard her anxiety, she could recognize her ego's yearning for approval. She didn't get approval from Gina. To get approval she had a couple of options. One option was to try to make nice with Gina and "fix" the situation. The other method Laura used often was to turn to her husband or best friend to soothe her and get her need for approval met through them, or at least try.

Laura decided to see her anxiety as a flag, telling her to instead take the path of self-approval and trust. She told herself that even if she had spoken "out of turn," she was definitely coming from love. She trusted that whatever was expressed was meant to be shared between her and Gina. Laura trusted Gina to do what would best serve her and her husband's highest good. Laura took the radical direction of choosing to let go of hanging on to Gina's reaction and marital conflict. Rather than worry, she refocused her energy on her goals and dreams.

When anxiety would pop up regarding Gina and whether everything was okay between her and her husband, Laura would let go by saying a prayer for their wellbeing and happiness. Two weeks went by and then Laura received a call. Gina expressed relief at having been able to express her deep shame. She also made a commitment to begin personal work to understand what was behind her affair and how she should approach it with her husband.

Laura admitted, "Talking to Gina was awkward, and I honestly didn't want to address her affair." She told me that without sensitivity to the higher- consciousness meaning of her anxiety, there was no way she would ever have talked to Gina. Now, all she could think of was the consequences of *not* sharing! "If I hadn't spoken with Gina, she'd still be carrying around so much shame and struggle. More importantly, it would likely have been years (if ever) before she sought support. Unconsciously, I'm sure I would be weighed down by guilt too. Plus, I now feel so empowered, having learned to approve of myself rather than look for approval from others after taking a risk." Laura continues to draw encouragement from this experience to trust in her inner wisdom for guidance as to when to take a risk and when to let go.

EXAMPLE #2 IRRATIONAL FEARS

Although Karen had advanced in her career as a surgeon during a time when women doctors became either ob/gyn doctors or pediatricians, she still struggled with wanting to be a good girl. In her career, she had no problem asserting herself. There she understood the playing field, and sharing her opinion was a vital part to her success.

Personal matters were a whole different story. Outside her job, Karen felt that she was constantly carrying around some level of anxiety. She feared she would unintentionally hurt someone's feelings, get things wrong, or that people simply would not like her. Even though she knew her anxiety was irrational, the smallest situation could ignite fear in her.

One such situation came up when Karen had an appointment to take her dog to the groomer. Unbeknownst to Karen, the groomer had a new sign-in procedure. When the groomer spoke to Karen about the new procedure, Karen was extremely embarrassed, causing her anxiety to kick into overdrive. The whole drive home, her anxiety would not stop berating her. *What an idiot you are. You should have known better. Cindy (the groomer) probably thinks you feel you're too good to follow the rules, or too unaware to have noticed the very conspicuous sign-in sheet.* When she arrived home, Karen tossed around the idea of writing to Cindy, calling her husband, or just throwing herself on a pillow to cry.

When we spoke, she admitted she knew how irrational the fears were that were driving her anxiety. Still, she could not seem to prevent this anxiety from taking over her mental state. We used the questions offered above to probe deeper into what was beneath her anxiety.

(Question #1) When I asked Karen what her fear was about this situation, she responded, "What I am afraid of is that Cindy may no longer like me. Even though my rational brain tells me not everyone can like me, I want everyone to not only like me, but to *really* like me."

(Question #2) I then asked Karen, "How do you feel when

you are not liked?" Karen revealed that if she thinks about not being liked, she feels extremely alone, scared, and overwhelmed.

(Question #3) I asked Karen what that scared part of her needs in that moment. Her response was, "When I think of myself being scared, alone, and overwhelmed, I feel like a little kid again. That little girl wants to be consoled and told everything will be all right. She wants to know someone can handle her."

(Question #4) When I asked Karen about the ego theme underneath her anxiety, she immediately knew that this was about her not being good enough! The scared part of her was afraid because she didn't feel safe being herself. She felt that she always had to be perfect, when she wasn't. She knew this part of her needed her support to be free to make mistakes, have needs, and not be on top of everything all the time.

(Question #5) How does your essence want you to take action to support this healing? Karen did not hesitate: "My essence wants me to give nurturance to myself, as I would my own daughter, when my fears are triggered. My essence also wants me to practice being more open and vulnerable. Doing so will give me the nurturance I always craved."

Karen made a note to pay attention to this little girl within her every time her anxiety was triggered. When something brought up any kind of fear, she would place her hand over her heart and start saying nurturing statements to herself. She also started sharing more of her needs and vulnerabilities within her interactions. Although it was scary at first, she immediately saw how doing this made her feel liked for *all* of who she is, rather than for only the "good and shiny parts," as Karen called them. Within a few weeks, the irrational fears Karen had carried with her for years suddenly vanished!

CLAIM THE GIFT OF ANXIETY!

Anxiety, coming from your ego, will always pull you into the past with sorrow and regret, or into the future with fear and worry. Your ego would have you believe that staying focused on the past or future keeps all the bases covered, giving you better control. The problem is, you have no real power in the past or future. The present moment is where you can have real impact in your life.

Your anxiety is summoned to call you back into the present moment, where you may take the necessary action now to create the future you desire. Anxiety means your action is required. You are being shaken to let go of the trappings of your mind, where the illusion of control and safety live, and instead choose to live from your heart. Within your heart, the illusion of control and safety are absent, yet this is the only truly safe way, because your heart leads you to fulfillment. Your rational mind cannot. Your anxiety signals you to get out of your head and back into your heart.

To get back to your heart, first get back into your body. Your body helps you become present, so dance, drum, or exercise, while listening for a rhythm. Go outside and stomp barefoot on the ground. Feel your heart's rhythm. That is the guidance your anxiety is calling you back to – your unique rhythm of life.

- Remember, the gift of anxiety is your signal that you are going in the wrong direction. Your anxiety is present so that you will ask yourself, "What does my heart want me to know, and how would my heart act? In other words, how would you act if you didn't believe in fear? This is the direction of your empowered self. The more you follow your empowered self's lead, the more you learn greater self-trust. The greater self-trust you have, the less you are swayed by fear.

Trust in the rhythm of your heart and allow yourself to be led on your journey by your empowered self. Imagine what it would be like to realize the opportunity being offered every time you felt anxious. Imagine how different your life would be if your thoughts, beliefs, and actions were the fruits of love, rather than fear. Your essence is calling you to live in deeper self-trust because the more you do, the more you live with confidence and courage to claim your most fulfilling life. Trust and use the gift of anxiety to take the action your empowered self is calling you to make!

F.E.E.L. FRUSTRATION

THE GIFT OF FRUSTRATION IS EXPANSION!

WHEN YOU HEAR THE WORD EXPANSION, WHAT COMES TO you? I think of growth and openness to greater possibilities. The word freedom comes to mind.

The reason you feel free when you expand is because you have successfully learned how to let go of another layer of your ego. The less control your ego has over your life, the freer you are to be you! As you know, your ego doesn't like expansion. The energy of your ego is just the opposite – contraction.

Contraction in and of itself is not necessarily bad. There are times when you need to contract in order to rebalance. The problem is that your ego wants you to stay contracted. It uses the illusion of safety to keep you contracted. While you believe you are staying safe, your ego plays you like a marionette through rigid, limiting, and controlling habits, thoughts, and beliefs. Unconsciously, you act this out as you stay wedded to a notion that there is only one "right" way to reach whatever it is you desire.

Fortunately, your natural instinct is to experience expansion. Some even say that the purpose of our existence is for each of us to be able to experience our most expanded version of self. In other words, your nature wants you to realize your fullest potential.

Your essence recognizes that you cannot open yourself to your fullest version of self or life when your viewpoint is too narrow. Frustration is the energy coming from your essence that urges you to move toward expansion. Your frustration does this by first allowing you to recognize you are limiting yourself. Otherwise, how would you know when your own mindset is getting in the way of your growth? Second, your frustration is present to open you up to discover that another way exists that will, in fact, work for you.

Believe in your ego and your frustration makes you the victim, yet again. Exhaustedly, your ego wails: "But I have tried everything! I don't know what I am doing wrong or what more I can do. I gave it my best." Your ego hopes that this kind of thinking will eventually wear you out to the point of giving up on having your desires met. Without understanding the higher-consciousness message, you have limited choices: give up, which will only lead to sadness and, ultimately, depression, or keep trying the same ol', same ol' while hoping for different results. Neither of these options serves you.

The higher-consciousness message of your frustration is telling you that another path exists. This path typically goes against what your rational mind thinks or perceives, as the way to get the results you desire. This path also often involves risk. The energy of frustration is there to support your willingness and courage to break out of the box your ego put you in, and instead expand.

Think of frustration as your rocket fuel. In order for a rocket to burst through the atmosphere (the rocket's current reality) and enter a new realm of space (the rocket's potential), tremendous energy is needed. The vast majority of the rocket's fuel is used in the first few minutes in order to break through the Earth's atmosphere. Your frustration carries the energy you need to break through the old ways of doing and thinking and instead choose a new way that goes beyond your comfort zone and into your potential zone!

PARADIGM SHIFT: FRUSTRATION IS CAUSED BY LACK OF PATIENCE?

Have you ever told someone who was frustrated to "take a breath" only to find them turning their frustration on you? Me too! Before I understood the higher-consciousness meaning to our feelings, I used to tell my husband all the time to "Just be more patient with yourself," whenever he became frustrated. Of course, this only frustrated him more. This is because he started off patient, and then gradually his patience grew thinner and thinner.

Because patience wears thin with frustration, we conclude that lack of patience is a major cause of our frustration. Actually, this is what your ego wants you to believe. You see, when you believe your lack of patience perpetuates frustration, you are to blame for your frustration. With focus on your lack of patience, you can't attend to the higher-consciousness meaning of your frustration. What the frustration is trying to tell you is that your expectations are based upon a false set of beliefs.

For instance, every time my husband is about to start a new house project, I know without a doubt that he is going to get frustrated. This is because he carries a deeply rooted belief about what a man should be able to fix around the house. When I didn't understand the higher-consciousness message of frustration, I would encourage him to keep trying by "just being more patient" and that eventually, he would get the job done. It simply wasn't true. Patience wasn't the cure-all. What patience usually led to was: a HUGE waste of time (according to my husband), and even putting his life in danger when an electric jolt knocked him on his ass! His ego version of his frustration would lead him to beat himself up because apparently, he lacked a talent that all other men worth their weight had, in spades.

The message from love, however, was just the opposite. His voice of love wanted him to realize that people aren't born with these skills based on their gender — they just learn them. My husband learned different skills growing up, therefore making the handyman process more foreign to him. Certainly, if it was truly his heart's desire to be able to fix things, he could learn. If he felt creativity or joy from working with his hands in that way, he would be guided to spend more and more time to learn the necessary skills.

What was really driving his need to be able to fix things on his own was his ego. His ego told him what a man should be capable of doing, which made my husband create expectations he could not immediately live up to. In his ego mind, there was an unrealistic chauvinist telling him: "I have a penis; therefore, I should automatically know how to fix most, if not all, complex household problems as they arise."

I know the feeling. I used to have the same belief about cooking. I would put tremendous weight on whether or not someone liked my cooking because my ego told me: "I have a vagina, which means I should naturally know how to cook." I didn't. Both my parents worked full-time jobs when I was growing up, which meant we ate a lot of take-out. What I had going for me, which my husband didn't have, was an out from my ego. My ego could hook on to a notion of being empowered by NOT being "chained to the kitchen." Yet, a time did come for me where I realized my essence wanted to cook and I really didn't know how. I hired a food coach, which at the time was considered a really odd thing to do, because after all, isn't cooking something you just sort of know? Not for me! Hiring a food coach was one of the best investments in my life because someone taught me how to cook the types of healthy foods I wanted to cook. Most of all, I do feel very feminine when I cook, as it is a process I truly enjoy and feels very aligned with my authentic expression.

In the case of my husband, frustration was coming through, as it always does, to give him a choice. His loving guidance wanted him to ask himself if he truly wanted to invest the time and money in himself to learn these skills, or pay someone else who had already invested in him/herself to learn. By asking himself this one question, he went from a limited expectation, based on the ego fear of not being a good enough man, to an expanded choice that defines and empowers how he wants to spend his time and money. This is what his frustration was really about — that he'd put himself in a box, which limited the way he defined himself as a valuable man. In the end, his frustration both healed and expanded his view and appreciation of himself, as well as others!

A FRUSTRATING STORY – HOW FRUSTRATION WORKS WHEN NOT UNDERSTOOD THROUGH LOVE

Kelly's dream, like so many others' dream, was to settle down, get married, and have children. She came to me filled with frustration because she was now forty-two and her dream seemed to be slipping away before her eyes. Even though she felt fortunate to be in a relationship with someone who loved her, he was unwilling to commit to marriage. In some ways, she reasoned, her partner was ideal. He supported her career, loved her unconditionally, and was completely trustworthy. They were best friends. And while she couldn't imagine ever leaving him, she was growing impatient about whether or not her dream would happen.

Kelly's frustration was present to tell her that by staying with Brandon, her dream would never happen. It's not because Brandon wouldn't marry her; eventually, if Kelly made an ultimatum, he would marry her. What Kelly's frustration was trying to tell her was that Brandon was not her ideal partner. In other words, even if they got married, she would not experience the intimacy, care, and passion she craved.

A part of Kelly knew the loving guidance of her frustration was right. She had convinced herself that the type of love she dreamed of didn't exist. Her rational mind reminded her of the other men she'd dated, men who were much worse than Brandon. Her ego was telling Kelly: "Brandon is the best you're going to get." Feeling this was her last shot at finally getting her dream fulfilled, she stuck with Brandon and convinced herself she just needed to be patient.

When I talked to Kelly, I wanted to know what fear-based messages were behind her staying with Brandon. She had many! First was the fear of feeling that she'd wasted too many years on Brandon NOT to have her dream realized by him. The second fear was of being alone. Even though Kelly was a very independent woman, living and thriving in Los Angeles, she feared she would be alone for the rest of her life. Her third big fear was the oh-so-familiar "What will people think?" When she was with Brandon, at least people figured they were going to get married. Without him, she would be single — again! Being single and never married at forty-two, she feared, would demonstrate just how unlovable she was.

BINGO! Being unlovable was Kelly's **core fear,** and her frustration was present to transform and ultimately expand her view of herself. Because she believed deep down that she was unlovable, she constantly tried to twist and contort herself to meet her partner's needs. She always tried to do her best to make the relationship work because she wanted her dream of kids and marriage to happen. In other words, she was convinced that the only way to get married was to forgo her own needs in order to meet the needs of another.

What her frustration was trying to show her was how her limited viewpoint, based upon the fear of being unlovable, would only continue to return the same results: men who reflected the belief that she wasn't worth the love she truly desired. This is how the Law of Attraction works. As long as Kelly believed parts of her were unlovable, she would experience not being fully loved. Her frustration was present to help her correct this imbalance and teach her to choose love for herself – her needs, desires, and dreams — over her fears.

Kelly understood that the loving message coming through her frustration was right. She could marry Brandon eventually, yet she would never be happy. A few weeks later, she made her choice to walk away from Brandon and open herself to experiencing the type of love she knew she truly desired AND deserved!

F.E.E.L. FRUSTRATION TO KEEP YOURSELF ON COURSE

If you've ever felt like you were spinning your wheels, you have felt frustration. The real pain of frustration is that you are sincerely trying to make something happen. Yet somehow, your efforts don't yield the desired results.

Wouldn't you know it! At this very moment as I write, I happen to be frustrated! I have been playing with the words in this section for an hour now and they aren't coming together as I would like. When I am in my ego regarding my writing, I get hung up on how much progress I want to make. I feel dissatisfied because my time and energy haven't resulted in what I have wanted to create.

All it took was for me to step away for (literally) two minutes, and I could hear the guidance of my essence. It reminded me of the narrow thinking my ego was engaging in at the moment. My ego wanted every word coming out on my computer to be the perfect, final copy. My ego wants results. My essence, on the other hand, knows my creative process. My essence desires connection, and connection through words may take more than a couple of trials. I am reminded to let go of my expectation of advancing further in my book. With expectations released, I can allow the words to come through me rather than forcing them. Within a matter of minutes, my whole mood shifts. This is because my sense of self reverts to my truth when I am no longer defining myself based upon my ego's expectations.

To shift out of frustration, you must be willing to let go of what you believe is the right way to get what you want. Your ego and rational mind conspire to have you believe definitive actions lead to specific results. If you want x, you must do y.

In some ways, the ego is correct. If I want to write a book, I must sit down and write. But where the ego takes over is in its constricted viewpoint about what writing should look like. My ego will brook no breaks, except for lunch, and fully expects creative, juicy ideas to constantly flow by staying glued to my computer for as long as the day permits. I tried that method only to find myself burned out and dissatisfied, even though I had written many pages.

Your essence, on the other hand, is there to breathe air into your life. This breath of fresh air allows movement, flow, and flexibility. Sometimes, it even calls you to take a step back!

To the rigidity of your ego, the guidance of your essence can feel downright scary. Your ego believes there is a "right" way, action, or path to get you to where you want to go.

Your rational mind judges all those actions being called from your essence as folly, with your not doing y resulting in your not getting x. In other words, **you don't know how to listen to your essence and still get what you want.** Your fear of not getting x keeps you aligned with your ego/rational mind and unknowingly compromises your highest version of self. So regardless of what your rational mind/ego tells you, you are still unable to realize your true desires in that way.

Frustration is your cue that you can trust your inner guidance far more than the limited view of your rational mind. This is not to discredit the rational mind in any way. Obviously, we all need to use logic. As a society, however, we have become overtrained in the use of rational, linear reasoning. Your negative feelings alert you to when your rational mind continues to be chosen over your essence. Frustration, in particular, is telling you that your rational mind/ego/logic is currently limiting you, and that there is another option available to you if you'll just open to another possibility.

Frustration also signals when you are allowing fear to over-power and devalue your true self. So many times I have heard people frustrated by their job, whether in the corporate world or in their work as a parent. They want this part of their life to be different because they know there is more potential there. Yet no matter what they try, the results don't work out as they planned or hoped. This is because their actions are based on fear rather than love.

The love emanating from your essence wants you to experi-ence your highest version of you. And for this to happen, you must act from love. You can't act from love, though, when you are buying into some limited belief about yourself. It is your ego that would have you believe you are so small and insignificant that there is no way you could make those "pipe dreams" in your heart your reality. You – the proverbial grain of sand on a vast beach — don't really matter, right? You don't have anything of value to offer, correct? You have a choice: sink into those thoughts OR listen to your essence scream "That's bullshit!"

Your essence is guiding you to realize that if you continue to choose your ego's narrow path, you guarantee an unfulfilled life of frustration. Or, as Henry David Thoreau more poetically said, "Most people lead lives of quiet desperation, and go to their graves with the song still in their heart." If you choose your true self over your ego in those moments of decision, you will find your frustration fueling you. With frustration as your fuel, you make a conscious choice to expand in ways you'd previously overlooked or fearfully avoided. This expansion leads to the realization of more and more of your potential.

HOW TO F.E.E.L. FRUSTRATION

Frustration signals that you are living a limited version of you. Your limited version of you is based on fear – fear of not being enough, not mattering, not being lovable, etc.... Your frustration is here to say ENOUGH! WAKE UP! It's time to expand your reality to include the highest, most authentic version of you. Frustration is present to inspire a shift in how you act, talk, and think when you know, honor, and accept the truth of every aspect of yourself.

Apply the Four Steps to Conscious Emotional Mastery (page 43) when frustration seems to come out of nowhere. For recurring patterns of frustration in a particular area of your life, you can use the questions below to go deeper and access the core shame themes that are limiting you.

1. What am I tolerating that isn't serving my highest good?
2. What reasons do I give for being tolerant, even though it does not serve my highest good?
3. How has my tolerance led to self-compromise?
4. What is the underlying fear that keeps me compromising myself?
5. What is the core shame that my fear is attempting to cover up by compromising myself?
6. How am I being asked not to compromise myself?
7. What action am I willing to commit to that honors rather than compromises myself?

EXAMPLE #1

Clarissa found herself taking way too long to write an email to a prospective new employer. She was getting more and more frustrated with herself because a part of her knew she was over-thinking what she had to say. Still, after two years at a dead-end job, she was feeling more desperate than ever to get out of her current line of work. The more she thought about her job, the more difficult writing this simple follow-up letter became. Rather than stay stuck, feeling frustrated and unhappy with her results, she decided to apply the Four Steps to Conscious Emotional Mastery.

When Clarissa focused on her ego, she heard harangues like: "You need to get this right, Clarissa. Your whole family is de-pending on you! Make sure you sound professional, but be sure to add humor, while also including your credentials. Clarissa, this is a great chance, so don't blow it!"

Clarissa then invited her essence to come through. As she focused on her heart, she got the sense that she was taking this email way too seriously. The feeling in her heart radiated how liked and valuable she truly was. Her essence seemed to be saying: "Keep this short and sweet, as you would for a business associate."

It all became clear: when Clarissa was listening to her ego, she was coming from a place of lack and desperation. Her essence, on the other hand, reminded her that at this point, she and the woman she was writing to were indeed business associates. Clarissa was simply in contact with a female associate she authentically liked. With this in mind, she was able to address her email from a place of self-value and equality. Remembering the truth of who she was, Clarissa was able to quickly shoot out a three-line email. Within minutes, she received a response. She could hardly believe her eyes when she realized she was being asked to go to lunch with the woman associate she liked AND the senior director, whom she had never met.

From this brief exercise, Clarissa could see how shifting out of the energetic tone of desperation enabled her to go to her natural state — warm, confident, and inviting. She truly believed that this difference in energy could be felt in the words she used in the email. She recognized how her frame of mind would be revealed whether she wanted it to or not. Fortunately for Clarissa, she used her frustration to understand how her desperate state was not working, and found loving guidance instead. Realigned with her natural state, she was now much more likely to attract a company that is her ideal!

EXAMPLE #2

Larry was a happy, positive guy. After really struggling as a kid, he was proud to say he was able to turn his life into a success. He had a wife, a son, and a job that brought in more money than he ever thought possible. Larry's only problem was that he wanted to feel passion! He was frustrated and bored by his job, even though it provided him a luxurious lifestyle.

Larry worked through the questions above to determine what was at the core of his frustration, and feeling passionless. When he asked himself the first question, right away he knew he was settling for a job he was completely bored with, staying only for the money. (The good old golden handcuffs!) He tolerated his job (Question #2) because his work afforded him a lifestyle he had grown accustomed to and, more importantly, really enjoyed.

As Larry reflected on Question #3, he was able to see how

putting up with his current work circumstances had led him to engage in behaviors that were not serving him. Feeling bored, he found himself drinking more, as a way to enliven his life. Even though the drunken euphoria never lasted, going out for drinks almost every night diverted his attention from how frustrated he was with his work. He had "settled" into staleness, and grown increasingly unhappy.

Larry's underlying fear (Question #4), which kept him stuck in his current position, was of being unable to find another job. His shame (Question #5) was about feeling he wasn't smart enough to get another high-paying job because he never finished college.

When Larry was stuck in his head, trying to figure out how to regain passion in his life, he assumed the only answer was to quit his current job. But when he asked his essence what it would look like for him not to compromise himself (Question #6), he realized what his essence really wanted. Larry's essence was **craving** to be challenged again.

Larry loved his work and was naturally very good at it. He wanted to take this work to the next level, but was afraid to throw his name into the ring to be considered for a higher position because a college degree was required. If "found out" by his company, Larry feared his associates would think less of him. Unbeknownst to him, he was unconsciously trying to hide from others judging him as an unintelligent, irresponsible person — words Larry often heard in his boyhood from his stepfather.

After processing the insight that came forward through this exercise, Larry knew exactly what he needed to do (Question #7). He went into his boss's office and told him he would like to be considered for the national manager position. Three months later, Larry got the job. He shared with me afterwards that his passion for work and life has returned because he feels challenged again. Reignited, he can now walk away from the boozing simply because drinking no longer feels interesting in his current reality. Even better, Larry's frustration enabled him to address and heal the forty-year-old wound of believing he wasn't smart enough or good enough to succeed!

CLAIM THE GIFT OF FRUSTRATION

Being human, you are going to get stubborn sometimes about your beliefs and behaviors. This happens to all of us because having a set way of being and doing can simplify life so that you are not constantly having to reinvent the wheel. The problem is, it becomes difficult to recognize when you are too narrowly focused. Rather than see the warning signs of your limited view, your ego turns frustration and disappointment into blaming other people or circumstances. Remain unaware, and you unconsciously sabotage your dreams.

Thank goodness you feel frustration, because that energy is present to tell you to stop unconsciously acting upon your fears and choose your inner guidance instead. Your fear sees danger, dead ends, and overall impossibility, while your essence knows exactly what you need to do. The question is: Are you willing to step outside the comfort zone of what you believe you know and instead do something which initially makes no sense to your rational mind? If you continue to say no, frustration will only grow, eventually turning into anger, depression, or anxiety until you are willing to trust.

- Never lose sight of the fact that your frustration is actually a gift. It reminds you to ask yourself: "In what ways am I preventing my empowered self from seeing and acting upon all the possibilities that await me?"

Frustration is present to underscore the confines of your ego so that you may choose the limitlessness of your essence instead. Frustration imparts energy, allowing you to remember the unlimited version of yourself and what that being came here to do. Through frustration, you find the gumption to choose the road less traveled. In doing so, you choose to surrender and allow the possibilities of life to flow through you. Claiming your frustration from love is where the endless possibilities of life are recognized.

F.E.E.L. GUILT

THE GIFT OF GUILT IS TO REDEFINE YOU!

LIFE CAN FEEL TRICKY AT TIMES. YOU HAVE DECISIONS AND choices, many of which pull you in opposite directions. A part of you may feel guided to handle a situation one way, while another part of you feels taking that direction isn't "the right thing to do." Worse yet is when you've already done something and are left second-guessing as to whether you made the best choice. Self-doubt creeps in and you wonder if you handled a situation "wrong." This inner tug-of-war is guilt.

The reason you feel so pulled in different directions when you are making a difficult decision, or feel guilt after you do, is that your ego and essence have two very different agendas. Guilt that runs on fear is concerned about consequences. Egoic guilt wants to know if there is a penalty, whether real or perceived, for your behavior. Guilt inspired by love, on the other hand, is guiding you to check in with yourself to see if you are acting on behalf of the highest expression of you.

Guilt from ego and guilt from love collide when acting from the highest version of yourself results in consequences you would rather not bear. (Yes, your essence WILL lead you to short-term outcomes you do not like, in order to create long-term results that are aligned with the highest good of all.) Any potential pain, whether short-term or not, kicks in your ego's efforts to keep you safe from the disappointment of not getting your needs met.

Remember, your ego is the protector of the part of you that feels vulnerable. And it uses guilt to get you back in line. Your ego knows that acting a certain way is more likely to get your needs are met. By triggering guilt, it helps you to avoid the pain of disappointment, or of feeling foolish for having tried and failed. If that means manipulating or sacrificing your true self in order to feel safe or good about yourself, then so be it.

The love expression of guilt is present to wake you up from a life on auto-pilot. Your fears keep you in a reactive mode, while your essence wants you to respond from your highest expression of authentic self. Guilt is present to awaken you from ways in which you are running on fear rather than love.

UNDERSTANDING GUILT

The reason guilt can be so darn confusing is because both ego and essence use the same language when they speak through your guilt. Both will ask, "What are you doing?" Your ego will be concerned about potential denial of a need's fulfillment. Even if this need is not completely fulfilled, your ego believes that something is better than nothing. Your essence, on the other hand, is showing you what you have to gain by letting go of what no longer serves you. Taking crumbs rather than experiencing true fulfillment never serves you as an adult. Your essence is urging you to reveal more of your brilliant self so that you may claim a life that makes your heart sing.

Let's take, for instance, feeling guilty about eating a piece of chocolate cake. In this scenario, you have just made a commitment to yourself three days earlier to eat healthier. You know when you eat healthy food that you feel more energized and better overall. At the same time, you feel powerless before the fudgy yumminess within inches of your mouth, enticing you. Temptation takes over and you give in to having a slice.

Right before you take that first bite, you hear your guilt saying, "What are you doing?" Your fear voice responds, "One piece won't hurt." (Your fear wants to keep you the same, because unconsciously you are apprehensive about claiming more of your potential, in this case, your health and all the associated benefits.) The loving voice of your guilt is guiding you to stop reacting to a piece of cake and respond in a way that will best serve you. In this case, the voice of love is saying, "What are you doing?" to remind you of your commitment to yourself and put down the cake.

Now let's say it's the same situation, and you feel guilty about eating a piece of cake. This time, however, you are the epitome of health. You have largely cut out processed foods and sugars from your diet, and are reaping the benefits of feeling energized and healthy. You feel that having something sweet occasionally is fine. The problem is that you never feel free to indulge completely guilt-free. Even at a special event, your guilt is on you to skip dessert. You hear it ask: "What are you doing? You don't want to go back to that big butt you can barely squeeze into your jeans, do you?" Your ego issues its warning: "Sweets are a slippery slope for you!"

As you have probably guessed, the critical voice judging your butt isn't coming from love. The love version of guilt is always about stopping you from reacting and instead learning to respond in alignment with your highest self. *Reactions* are based on fear, whereas *responses* can be based on love, if you consciously choose.

The higher-consciousness version of guilt is showing you how you are unconsciously defining yourself as a person who must be uptight and restrictive to maintain your health. Your essence is triggering guilt in the interest of reframing your definition of health. It is there to remind you that too much self-denial leaves no room for joyful, pleasurable eating from time to time. This time your guilt is asking you to stop reacting to cake in an acetic way and incorporate pleasure in eating as another crucial component to health as well.

Notice that in both cases, guilt is present to bring you back into balance. Balance is found from within by determining what choice serves your overall good. The truth is, we all tend to see ourselves too one-dimensionally. We unknowingly engage in black-and-white thinking that limits who we are.

If you're more likely to find yourself in the first scenario, you may have an image of yourself as someone who perhaps isn't completely healthy, but at least enjoys life. It goes almost without saying that if you continue to indulge in a way that isn't healthy, you aren't going to feel happy, because your overindulgence is based on fear. If you can picture yourself better in the second scenario, you may have an image of yourself as someone who is able to meet goals or adhere to personal standards. You attribute this to having self-control or discipline. The problem is that the self is overly controlled when there's so little room for the flexibility or pleasure you would like. Neither scenario is balanced, which is why guilt comes into play. Guilt is indicating that your self-image is not in sync with the truth of who you are. Your guilt wants you to shed another layer of ego identity to more fully recognize your true, naturally balanced self.

PARADIGM SHIFT: USE GUILT TO KEEP YOU OUT OF LINE INSTEAD OF IN LINE!

In the emotional Stone Age, guilt warns of misdeeds, and is generally commensurate with the perceived degree of wrongness. According to the unspoken rules of reactive guilt, whenever it appears, you should automatically stop what you're doing and instead make the "right" choice. In other words, guilt is present to keep you in line!

Do you ever wonder if the line you are "toeing" is the line you wish to stay in? Lines aren't altogether bad. They keep us organized and can help get our needs met. The problem is that we end up sleepwalking in lockstep, because that is what we know. Guilt, coming from ego, is going to scream at you to get back into line the second you even *think* about stepping out of bounds. Guilt from your ego pushes you to find your own guidance as to whether the line you're in remains a good fit for you.

What exactly are these lines I am talking about? They are the roles you play in your life. Common roles include the behaviors and attitudes involved in being a woman/man, daughter/son, mother/father, friend/lover/spouse, employee/employer, and the meaning you attach to these roles. The stronger you identify with a certain role or roles, the more standards there will be. You will use adjectives such as devoted, smart, funny, strong, financially stable, etc., to judge whether you are adequately fulfilling your role or not.

Emblazoned in your mind are ideas or notions of the standard you should be living up to in order to truly fulfill your role. Of course, you will never be able to live up to the standard.

See for yourself what expectations you may have for yourself by doing this quick exercise.

1. List the roles that describe you.
2. List the qualities that would help you to be your best in the roles you mentioned. (How do you desire to come across to others in your role/s? What actions do you expect of yourself in this role? How are you supposed to feel or think in your role?)
3. Carefully examine the list you have created and write down how these expectations, outlined in Question 2, are running your life.

My guess is that your list was long and wide. Subconsciously, in the recesses of your mind, your ego is constantly judging you against your list. Through guilt, your ego uses your list to put you back in your place. It tells you that if you want to be defined as a good enough (fill in the role), you better abide by this list. And the more you abide, the more exhausted you are.

Your essence, on the other hand, uses guilt to jar you into seeing how you are being run by something other than your truth. Guilt, from the standpoint of your essence, is there for you to recognize how the unattainable ideal self that you strive to be is detracting from your inner peace and joy. Guilt is your opportunity to determine if you want to fall back in line with all the rules and standards of your ego, or instead give room for your essence to BE.

At this point, you may be wondering, "Doesn't everyone want to strive to be their best? What's wrong with having standards?" The answer is absolutely nothing, IF your version of your best self is truly aligned with your highest expression of you. Oftentimes, however, your "best self" is defined by your ego's version of success or happiness, which ultimately will not be fulfilling or joy-filled for you.

The fact of the matter is that sometimes your ego and essence can want the same goal for you. The difference between the two is how that goal is defined and attained.

An easy way of awakening from the ego's trickeries coming from guilt is to listen for the "shoulds." Stop "shoulding" yourself to death! If you listen to your internal dialogue when your guilt is triggered, all you will hear is: "I really ought to have done..." or "Am I a bad person because I didn't..." .

What you want to be listening for behind those shoulds is how you believe you fell short of a certain standard. Remember, each time you feel guilt, it's an opportunity to ask yourself: "What am I buying into about who I think I should be?" Then ask yourself if this "should" fits with your highest version of self in this specific circumstance.

Believe me, the shoulds are always there, especially when you are calling on more of your potential to be expressed. This is because you often have to let go of who you once were to become the person you are meant to be. When you listen to love's version of guilt, you are recalling who you really are. Go within, and hone in on what feels in alignment with the highest version of yourself.

If you were that version of yourself that soars, what would you want and how would you respond? This is your highest version of self, poised to come forward. Guilt will support you in making radical shifts in how you define, perceive, and act as you impeccably align with your essence.

A GUILTY STORY: GUILT AND INFERTILITY

Rita had been trying to get pregnant for years, when she sought out support. She had tried everything possible, from traditional doctors to herbs and acupuncture. Still she could not get pregnant. She was ANGRY, yet back of her anger was a huge amount of guilt she carried for being unable to get pregnant.

Rita confided that she completely blames herself for her inability to conceive. Spewing from her mouth was reason after reason as to how she had screwed up her dream of becoming a mother due to her earlier life choices. At the top of her list was making work her top priority, and relationships second, which is what led to her first divorce. By the time Rita married a second time, she was much older. She believed she had wasted her "fertility years" selfishly. Drugs, alcohol, smoking, eating unhealthy foods, and workaholic behavior had been her lifestyle. Now, Rita felt that she was paying the inevitable price.

As Rita shared detail after detail of "the facts" of what she'd done "wrong," all I could hear was deep self-hatred. She was defining herself based on her past and not at all based on the person she is today – a healthy, loving, and committed woman. Rita's guilt was calling her to acknowledge, honor, and love herself rather than blame, hurt, and demean herself.

As she worked to redefine herself, what she saw was a little girl who felt alone and afraid. Inside her was an emptiness that she had tried to fill in every which way – drugs, alcohol, food, gossip. Finally able to see what she had been trying to ignore her whole life, she changed her focus. For the immediate future, her attention was no longer riveted on trying to get pregnant. Her self-prescribed task was to learn how to fill the emptiness from within herself. Rita did, and a newfound peace came over her life. She was finally able to forgive herself and others, and let go.

Her newfound love for herself inspired her to eventually try a different assisted reproductive technology. She was going to give herself one last shot to try to get pregnant. Fortunately, this time the outcome was different. She became pregnant and had a beautiful, healthy baby girl. Rita attributes her successful pregnancy to being willing to use her guilt to redefine herself from love, rather than the former fear, hatred, and lack.

F.E.E.L. GUILT TO KEEP YOURSELF ON COURSE

Guilt is present from the standpoint of love to have you stand up for your true self. All you need to do when you feel guilty is to be very conscious of the version of yourself that you are choosing to be. To be conscious, close your eyes and be clear about the quality of person wanting to come through your heart. Is this person open or closed, trusting or fear-filled, honest or manipulative? What is the person you desire to be in this situation?

Saying you want to be a good person is not enough of a definition. Being good isn't always as black or white as it first appears. This is why so many people, especially women, struggle with always trying to be "good."

A classic example may be found in confrontations. Most people who want to be viewed as good try to avoid confrontations like the plague. What they'll tell themselves is: "I just don't want to hurt anyone." Their ego will have them believe that avoiding the confrontation is good. It will assure them: "This way, no one will get hurt."

When you sidestep a confrontation, what you are often trying to avoid is getting hurt *yourself.* Unknowingly, you are really guarding against not getting your own needs met by another. You are seeking validation that you are indeed a good person. From past experiences, you learned that being good was most likely to win approval and attention.

The problem is, what feels good to another person may not be good for you. For instance, it may feel great to your partner that you take care of all the household chores, while it may not be good for you. At first, you share how the household setup is too much of a strain on you. When your spouse retorts that he is even more stressed, trying to keep the family financially afloat, you back down immediately. Your shame button has been pressed because you fear that you are acting selfishly. The only way to prove your unselfishness is to be more giving. Wanting to be the good, supportive, loving wife, you fall back into line doing what works for your spouse but not for you. For the time being, you get to feel like you are being a good person because you have chosen the route deemed as "unselfish." Over time, however, your resentment builds, leaving both you and your spouse feeling unfulfilled in the marriage.

So are you really being a "good" person for backing away from how you feel and falling back into line? If you look at the long-term results, you will find nothing good about the outcome. No one is happy. How good can that be?

Hold on to your seats, because here's the irony: Trying not to be selfish is actually quite selfish. It is selfish of you not to use your power, your insight, and your love to heal aspects of your relationship that are broken. Your holding back foments unhealthy energy within your marriage and your family, should children be involved. Rather than model how differences may be resolved in a way that works for everyone, you unconsciously teach your children the win-lose model.

The kicker is that you unconsciously perpetuate unhealthy patterns in your marriage in order to receive the validation and affirmation you crave. How selfish is that? You are willing to make your marriage and family life suffer, just so you can feel that you are a good person. It's crazy, but many of us fall into this subtle trap when the ego is running us.

Again, when you're unconscious of it, guilt triggers shame, and shame pushes you back into line. When you feel guilt from the ego, you are afraid you are acting in cahoots with your shameful self rather than your ideal self. At the same time, as it becomes apparent that these "shameful" aspects in fact serve you, your essence uses guilt to help you release the judgments you hold against yourself. Though hidden and denied, these seemingly shameful parts of you have needs. But because they are viewed with shame, they must sneak behind your back to have their needs met. Unbeknownst to you, your shame creates unhealthy situations to satisfy those needs. This is why in the above example of trying to be unselfish, you unconsciously are being extremely selfish. The need has to be met in one way or another.

In the past, you would have likely remained unconscious of your shame's needs. Without understanding what it wants, you remain clueless as to why you are challenged in so many ways. However, once the shameful component is integrated into your sense of self, this particular "shame button" is gone, and guilt is no longer triggered in the same predictable ways.

Your essence wants to heal this split, once and for all, between the essential you and what you judge yourself to be. Spurred on by guilt, your essence encourages you to find what is true and right for you. You harbor opposites within you for a reason. You are both generous and selfish, loving and withdrawing, compassionate and indifferent. You are all, yet your ego wants to honor only that which it judges as good.

When you disown one side, guilt will urge you to address what you find shameful about yourself. You make shameful that which you believe others would judge about you, if they only knew the "truth" about who you really are. Attending to the loving guidance of your guilt, you are led to an inner shift from attachment to how others may judge you, to honoring all aspects of yourself. The result is that your outward actions are no longer based on fear. Instead, your actions come from believing in your inner knowingness, regardless of how that looks to others.

HOW TO F.E.E.L. GUILT

When you feel guilt, your higher consciousness is asking you to question whether living in alignment with your authentic and highest self is worth it to you. Are you willing to honor your own identity? Or will you continue to create a persona, based on others' expectations and approval, in order to temporarily feel you are okay, worthy, or good enough? Guilt gives you the choice of remaining the actor, doing your best to fill a role, or creating your own starring role based on open-hearted living that gives you the greatest fulfillment.

Guilt is your message to awaken from the ways that have been prescribed for you, and/or that you have used to define yourself. Some of these definitions may have been meant to support you, such as when you heard that you are so smart or so pretty. But ego knows how to take even the most positive of messages and use them against you to define yourself in a limited way. Your ego becomes so attached to and identified with such images that there is no room to breathe.

For instance, if you are the pretty one, you feel so defined by your looks that you may become obsessed and judgmental about your appearance. Of course, being judgmental of yourself leads to judging others. The resulting guilt is not to tell you what a bad person you are (more criticalness toward self), but instead to inspire you to redefine yourself without such negativity.

Other times, you have heard comments that hurt you, and used those to define yourself as well. You believe you are incapable or irresponsible because when you were young, people told you as much. What you learned is: "No matter how hard I try, the results are never good enough!" This leads you to give up on yourself or stop trying. A part of you feels guilty giving up, while another part of you feels relieved. In those cases, guilt is present to awaken you to how you are buying into a negative role that isn't serving you, and instead act from what your essence desires to create out of your life.

The challenge of guilt is that it often runs deep into our psyche, holding onto our shame with a firm grip. Utilizing the Four Steps to Conscious Emotional Mastery can loosen the grip (page 43). To uncover the shame theme coming from your guilt, ask yourself the following:

1. What do I feel guilty about?
2. How do I respond to the guilt? (i.e., cave in, defend my position, etc.)
3. What messages of shame do I carry about the guilt I feel?

4. How may this shamed part of myself actually be beneficial in certain circumstances?

5. What am I afraid I would lose if I expressed the beneficial side of my shame?

6. In what way does my role become redefined as I listen to the guidance of my essence and incorporate the beneficial aspects of my shame?

7. What action am I willing to commit to and take to begin to redefine my role?

EXAMPLE #1

For years, Samantha had used every new method available to quit smoking. But success was only temporary, and she was becoming more and more concerned about her health. With her fortieth birthday a few months off, she realized she was not the version of herself she desired. Not only was she still smoking but she had also packed on thirty pounds and was drinking more than she knew she should. Samantha was tired of the guilt she felt every time she found herself smoking again. She wanted to get to the bottom of why her habits had pulled her away from being the person she knows she can be.

Through learning the F.E.E.L. process, Samantha realized that her guilt was showing up to show how she was reacting, rather than responding. Samantha began to listen to and scrutinize all the reasons her ego gave for making it okay every time she lit up another cigarette. At first, this was tricky because the ego's reasons felt like facts, not excuses. To differentiate between her ego's voice and her inner voice, Samantha decided to give credence only to those messages that supported her goal of quitting smoking.

Here's what her ego shared: Stress was to blame. Samantha did indeed feel stretched too far with responsibility. The problem was that there was another layer of guilt keeping her maxed out for too long.

The deeper guilt, which weighed most heavily on her, had to do with caring for her aging parents. Fortunately, they were healthy. The problem was, neither of them could drive any longer. This meant groceries, doctor visits, and all random errands had to be provided by Samantha.

Her parents also still lived in the same house for over forty years. This meant lawn maintenance in summers and shoveling in winters. Each and every one of these duties, Samantha took upon herself to do, even though she was a chiropractor with a full-time practice.

Although she was exhausted by everything she was doing, she didn't feel she had a choice. She felt too guilty not to help her parents. But no matter how hard she tried, she still felt guilty for not doing more for them. F.E.E.L. to the rescue! Samantha realized that her ego was telling her that in order to be a good daughter, she needed to be doing everything she possibly could to help her parents as they age. After all they had done to support her, it was now her turn to fully support them. Yes, this made her life more challenging, but at least she could enjoy a close relationship with them. Plus she could continue to feel good, knowing they know how loved they are.

After her ego had more or less rested its case, Samantha called upon her essence. Because her ego was still making such a racket, she had to hunker down and focus on her heart to hear it speak. What came to her first was ego's insistence that she be the "good daughter." Her essence then presented the long list of all that was required to be the "good daughter," suggesting that she write it down. Samantha was shocked by what was coming up. Her essence then asked her to add to her list all that she expected of herself from her roles at work and at home with her daughter and husband. Now it became very clear to her why she was turning to cigarettes, food, and alcohol. She needed some way to "escape" these self-imposed responsibilities of trying to be good — even excellent — in all areas of her life.

Samantha's essence then gave her a visual of what it would look and feel like to switch from following her parents' lead to becoming her family's leader. This meant hiring help for the yard, even though her parents would prefer that Samantha do the job (since she could do it exactly the way they liked it). Samantha also needed to be willing to tap her other family members, such as her brother and sister, into service. Her sister actually lived closer to her parents than Samantha did, yet somehow, Samantha let her sister off the hook for helping out more. Her brother lived out of state, but he could contribute more financially.

As this new vision came into sharper focus, Samantha knew her family would reject her ideas at first. She didn't care. In fact, as she saw what needed to happen, she actually became angry. For the first time, she saw how trying to define herself based on her role of being the smart and responsible one was ruining her health. Samantha stuck up for her needs, and eventually the family began to work together.

The result was almost beyond imagining! Not only did Samantha stop smoking and drinking, but she also lost weight, Just as surprisingly, old familial patterns that no longer worked were adjusted and healed. Samantha confided, "With my father being 86 years old, I never would have expected change out of him, yet he has changed! These adjustments in responsibility have enabled him to finally let go and relax. Plus, my brother and sister and I are all getting along better than we have in years! I've even let go of more responsibility at work and given it to an intern — something I would never have considered previously. Best yet is that I now take half-days on Fridays that are just for me! I'd been afraid of delegating because I thought it would mean I wasn't doing a good enough job. Now I realize that being a good leader is seeing others as just as capable as I am and empowering them! Thank goodness for my guilt!"

EXAMPLE #2

Nina had been working for her friend Lisa for nine years, when she contacted me. Nina told me she was ready for a life change and wanted to quit her job. The problem was that she felt extreme guilt in doing so because her boss was also her best friend.

Nina and Lisa met in nursing school. Lisa went on to get her nurse practitioner's degree, which allowed her to open her own practice. Lisa created the practice with the agreement that Nina would be her right-hand woman. Lisa became both office manager and nursing assistant for the practice. After a few years, the practice took off.

Less than a year ago, Lisa had a baby, which left Nina more or less running the whole facility. Even though Nina desperately wants out of the practice, she feels too guilty to tell Lisa. When Lisa comes in to work for a couple of hours each day, she is unhappy with Nina's work. At times, Lisa has called Nina lazy and incompetent. Nina is tired of the emotional abuse and the extra work she has taken on since Lisa had her baby. She doesn't want to hurt her friend, but at the same time can no longer take feeling miserable every day she goes to work.

I took Nina through the in-depth questions to help her get to the core of her guilt, which would give her clarity.

(Question #1) The thought of quitting flooded Nina with guilt because she knew she would be leaving her best friend high and dry at a time when she needed her most.

(Question #2) At first, Nina tried to handle the extra responsibility by assuming that the shift was temporary. But when she began to see there was no end in sight, she asked Lisa to hire more help. Lisa's responses made Nina feel selfish and lazy.

(Question #3) Nina felt shame as she questioned whether she really was being selfish and lazy. She wondered if she might be jealous that Lisa had created a practice, married, and had a baby, something Nina dreams of for herself. Most of all, she feared she was being lazy by not wanting to help out her friend more.

(Question #4) At first, Nina rejected the possibility of any benefit to being selfish and lazy. We then talked about times when she had done something just for herself. She admitted that she always likes to take the best, cheesiest piece of pizza and chooses first, even before her nieces and nephews. She always felt guilty about doing this because she thought a good person would let kids choose first. When I asked her if her nieces and nephews seemed to care, she said they'd never complained once.

I asked Nina how it would feel to allow herself to grab that first piece without guilt and she said, "Wow, that would feel incredible. It would feel like I'm being nice to myself, even treating myself. It would be nice to allow my desires to come first!"

Bingo! The floodlights went on in Nina's mind. Being selfish allows you to take care of your needs! Simultaneously, she could also see how being lazy enables you to relax. The way Nina was currently living, her needs came dead last, which meant she never had time to relax. She could see how being more selfish and lazy might actually be to her advantage, but her guilt always stopped her. Her need to be selfish was exposed in the seemingly trivial matter of a slice of pizza. This showed that she really needed to be much more focused on self-care, care that she doesn't feel weird or sneaky about.

(Question #5) I continued by asking Nina what she feared might be lost by expressing the beneficial side. Nina went deep within for a few moments and recalled how she'd felt when she showed these sides of herself when she was little. Her fear was that these disowned aspects of herself made her unlovable. She believed that if she showed and acted on these desires, even if they benefited her, she would be rejected, and ultimately be alone.

(Question #6) When Nina thought about how her essence would redefine her role by incorporating these presumably shameful wishes in a healthy manner, she saw a completely different person. Nina's view of her role then shifted from trying to make Lisa happy to making *herself* happy by listening to her needs and making them a priority.

Nina's ego had led her to believe that ignoring her own needs would *earn* her the love and respect she desired from others. But listening to her ego's interpretation of guilt made her feel incredibly alone and unlovable. Nina wanted back her friendship, where she and Lisa could have fun. Nina wanted to feel happy, not resentful. Her fear was that if she shared her needs, the relationship would collapse and they would no longer be friends. The truth was that the relationship had already imploded, and neither of them was happy.

(Question #7) Nina made a commitment to talk to Lisa within a week, to tell her she wanted out of the practice, and why. Her fear was still present that they might never speak again. What Nina feared more, however, was continuing in a job she no longer enjoyed.

A week later, Nina talked to Lisa. Lisa was devastated, and screamed at Nina about how selfish she was being, especially while her child was so young. Nina acknowledged how difficult it had been for both of them. At the same time, she knew this was no longer working. Nina left and didn't hear back from her friend for months.

At first, Nina was devastated that their friendship had ended on such a terrible note. The first few days after their break, Nina would become overwhelmed with guilt, worrying about what would happen to Lisa and her practice. During those times, she would check in with her essence. Even though Nina felt incredibly sad and alone when her guilt cropped up, she also felt free of the chains that had kept her stuck in a role she no longer wanted. She used the F.E.E.L. process to listen to the loving message of her sadness. In doing so, each day Nina became stronger and clearer about the life she wanted to lead. Within a few short months, Nina had changed. She lived with clear boundaries and intentions. And the change was paying off, as she landed a job she loved and started dating again.

Four months later, Nina got a call from Lisa, apologizing. Lisa could now see how she had been disrespectful of Nina and taken advantage of their friendship. Slowly they began to reconnect, yet under different terms. Even though their reconnection took time and patience, Nina is happy that her guilt allowed her to redefine her response to life according to her essence, rather than her ego. She has found that by incorporating those aspects she once deemed shameful, people have the opportunity to truly connect with the real Nina. She no longer feels alone and, more importantly, she feels loved in her relationship for the person she truly is — needs and all!

CLAIM THE GIFT OF GUILT

Depending on which interpretation we listen to, guilt can give us the opportunity to free ourselves or remain bound. Listen to guilt from the voice of your ego and you'll stay stuck in a faux you that does not serve you or anyone else. Listen to guilt from the voice of love, and you break free from the ego-fortification that is little more than a holding cell.

Think of it this way: Without guilt, you would not be aware of your identification with the habits, beliefs, and past mistakes you unconsciously use to define yourself. **Guilt, when understood through love, is a game-changer.** Guilt gives you the inspiration to envision the type of person you'd like to be, recognize the fear preventing you from being this ideal self, and take bold action to better align yourself with that truth. Allowing your guilt to guide you in this manner, you become the person you know you are meant to be.

- Remember, the gift of your guilt is that it inspires you to ask yourself: "In what ways am I denying who I truly am?" This is how you claim another layer of your empowered self.

Redefining yourself in a way that's much closer to the essential you – who you really are — takes guts and gusto! Admitting when you've done something against your core self, or recognizing how your way of being no longer serves you, is brave. Following the higher-consciousness message of guilt takes courage as you look within and find what is true and right for you. Whenever you feel guilt, use it as the signal it is meant to be, a time to redefine yourself from love rather than fear!

THE LIST

IN THIS CHAPTER YOU WILL FIND A LIST OF OVER FIFTY EMO-tions, emotions I call "derivative emotions." They are called derivative emotions because at the core of a particular feeling is an element of sadness, anger, anxiety, frustration, or guilt. This is good news! All it means is that you only need to know how to work with five feelings in order to be emotionally conscious.

The derivative emotions listed below will help you to identify a more specific message tied to the theme of one or more of the "Big Five" feelings. I will then share with you the common ego message associated with a particular feeling, as well as the empowered self's message. Sometimes, recognizing the guidance in the message coming from your empowered self will be enough to inspire action based on what you are feeling from love. At other times, you will need to go back and work with one or more of the Big Five to get clearer as to how you are being asked to move forward from a higher-consciousness perspective.

The empowered self's messages offered here are meant to be a fit for the majority of times you experience that particular feeling. Of course, you may occasionally intuit that the empowered self's message does not feel like a match with what you are experiencing. If this is the case, try looking up another feeling that is similar, or go directly to one of the five core emotions.

Without further ado, here is The List!

Abandoned: Derivative of Sadness

Ego Message: I am completely and utterly alone. I am not understood or loved for who I am.

Empowered Self's Message: You have abandoned your true self. You have chosen your ego over your essence to the point where you no longer know who you truly are. This separates you from your truth and your connection with God/Higher Power/Universe. The intensity of this pain works to help you recognize that your false self does not serve you. Listen without judgment, immediately, to your sadness.

Aggressive: Derivative of Anger

Ego Message: I want to take out my anger on someone or something.

Empowered Self's Message: You feel out of control because you believe you are powerless in this situation. This false belief makes you willing to compromise your integrity by lashing out in order to gain release from tension. The tension is present to push you beyond your normal limits, beyond what you are usually comfortable with doing, and seek deeper in your heart for resolution. You always have power. This power may be in learning from this situation to take fuller responsibility for your needs and personal boundaries. Claim your power through your highest version of yourself, rather than continue to react from fear.

Alone/lonely: Derivative of Sadness

Ego message: I don't have the connection with others that I crave to experience.

<u>Empowered Self's Message:</u> Your essence is directing you to go within to acknowledge, honor, and nurture your spiritual self's needs and desires. In other words, your empowered self feels disconnected from you. Your attention seems to be everywhere but on your true needs, desires, and wants, likely because a part of you feels unworthy. Give your inner self the deep nurturing attention that it loves. Through realigning with your truth, you not only deepen your relationship with yourself, but also open yourself more to others in the process.

Annoyed: Derivative of Frustration

<u>Ego Message</u>: I feel irritated by this situation/person.

<u>Empowered Self's Message:</u> Your annoyance is a twofold opportunity. First is to reaffirm what your healthy boundaries should be in these kinds of situations. Second is to determine why a situation or person has gotten "under your skin." This is your opportunity to recognize your internal hot button, which is an area of vulnerability. You feel vulnerable because you struggle with aspects of yourself that you don't want to accept. Whatever is annoying on the outside (i.e., a judgmental friend, a person taking too long in line etc.) is also within you and needs acknowledgment. What judgments does it bring up in admitting that this annoyance also exists in you? It is time for you to recognize and validate this quality's healthy expression.

Apprehensive: Derivative of Anxiety

<u>Ego Message:</u> I am afraid to make a move. I am doubtful things will work out in my favor. I don't want to make a fool of myself. It feels safer to hold back.

<u>Empowered Self's Message:</u> Like an animal that "freezes" in fear at any perceived threat, your ego is having you cling to the illusion of safety in stasis. The question you must ask yourself is whether your desire for safety is creating the fulfillment you desire. The energy of apprehension is present for you to use in taking a risk on behalf of your highest good. Rather than looking to the external to tell you whether your inner guidance is a good idea, you are being asked to trust and let go of expectations. You are always being supported on your path.

Ashamed: Derivative of Guilt and Sadness

<u>Ego Message:</u> I have acted in a way that confirms I am not as good of a person as I would like to be. Others see me in a way I am ashamed of.

<u>Empowered Self's Message:</u> Your essence is asking you to integrate aspects of yourself you judge as wrong. Your rejection of these aspects makes you distrust yourself. How are these parts of you there to support you? What does their healthy expression look and feel like? Consciously choose to allow them to be expressed, and you will more deeply honor the truth of all that you are.

Arrogant: Derivative of Anxiety and Sadness

<u>Ego Message:</u> I believe I am better in some way than another or others.

<u>Empowered Self's Message:</u> You are craving acknowledgment right now. You are turning to others and trying to show off your gifts in hopes of healing the fear that you don't matter. You are puffing yourself up in hopes that this protective

armor will conceal how much you feel your gifts and talents are undervalued, or perhaps not as great as you'd hoped. Learning to acknowledge and honor ourselves for who we are as spiritual beings reminds us all that there is no need to take ourselves so seriously. You are being called not to honor yourself based on external accomplishments, but instead for the huge heart and, up to now, unexpressed beauties that live within you. This serves to reground and sensitize you to the exquisitely simple joys of living.

Bored: Derivative of Frustration and Anxiety

Ego Message: My life feels incomplete, or that something is missing.

Empowered Self's Message: Boredom coming from your essence is an indicator that now is your time to expand. A part of you is trying to identify yourself based on the external. The sense of emptiness you feel, however, can only be filled from the inside. Let go of the false sense of safety found in your boredom and take a risk. Now is the time for action, no matter how small or big. Create, act, and move without judgment.

Confused: Derivative of Anxiety and Frustration

Ego Message: I feel pulled in too many directions. I don't know what I am supposed to do.

Empowered Self's Message: You are ego-tripping! Your ego is muddying the waters as a way to cast distrust over your inner wisdom. It does this through self-doubt, making you believe something is a much bigger deal that it actually is, or by creating a sense of urgency when there doesn't need to be one. Use the signal of confusion to care for your essence by engaging in activities that take you out of your head. Don't fall for your ego's claim to fame – that everything can be figured out in your head – or you'll end up changing your mind once you reconnect to your essence. Save time by clearing your head now, and reconnecting with your body, nature, and your heart.

Deceived: Derivative of Sadness and Anger

Ego Message: I have been taken advantage of by another. I am hurt, in disbelief, and feel betrayed.

Empowered Self's Message: You feel victimized, but you absolutely still have power. Your power is to use the deception as fuel to better protect yourself in the future. Being deceived allows you to see where you may have turned away from your truth due to the lure of the ego. Your ego may have had you believing everything was okay because a part of you wanted to believe so. What happens is you unconsciously (or consciously) end up ignoring warning signs coming from your inner wisdom. Use deception to empower yourself to claim clearer boundaries from love, rather than fear. In love, you no longer worry about looking ridiculous (or fear the loss of whatever your ego believes you would lose) when you question in order to find true clarity to make wise decisions for your highest self.

Detached: Derivative of Sadness

Ego Message: I don't feel connected to much and don't feel much of anything. At times, I feel empty.

Empowered Self's Message: Your ego is helping you to detach

from your pain, which feels safe because it is, at least, known. The reality is that you are detaching from your inner truth and wisdom, which creates elongated pain (a.k.a. suffering). The empty energy found in detachment is guiding you to recognize how the external can never fill an internal need. You are denying your internal world because it feels too scary to address. Now is your chance to reawaken to your inner wisdom and trust in the changes your heart wants you to make. Even if they are challenging in the short term, you will vitalize your life in the long term. Act from your heart to experience an immediate shift.

Disappointed: Derivative of Sadness

Ego Message: I feel let down. An experience did not work out as I had hoped or planned. I do not feel supported.

Empowered Self's Message: You are judging the situation from a short-term perspective based upon your expectations. You are being called to let go and trust. Trust that your needs will be fulfilled in the long run, even if this seems quite improbable based on the immediate results you received. Ask yourself in what ways the situation will help you to evolve. What more may you be preparing yourself to receive in the long term?

Disgust: Derivative of Anger

Ego Message: I am appalled and feel repelled.

Empowered Self's Message: You are being notified that something is not acceptable to you. This energy is present to support you in making changes within yourself, your family, community, or world that better serve all involved. If your change is run by your ego, the energy is contracting, limiting, and judgmental. If your change comes through your essence, the energy feels expansive and creates "soul-utions."

Doubtful: Derivative of Sadness and/or Guilt

Ego Message: I am second-guessing myself. I don't believe things will work out favorably. I hear a lot of "yeah, buts" in my head.

Empowered Self's Message: Doubt is present to indicate when you are giving more of your energy over to your ego rather than your internal truth. Ask yourself what message you received which ignited a fear and brought up your self-doubts. What message did you buy into about yourself that reinforces fear? Your essence is using your doubt so that you may feel urgency to drop an old story that no longer serves you and create a new story that does fulfill you. Allow doubt to be your warning that you are wrapping yourself back up in the comfort of the old rather than opening yourself to the new experiences your heart craves.

Dread: Derivative of Anxiety and/or Guilt

Ego Message: I don't want to do what I feel impelled to do. The thought of doing what I am about to do makes me sick.

Empowered Self's Message: Your inner wisdom is signaling to you that you are being called to make a significant shift. Many times you'll feel safer not making this shift because it involves letting go and trusting, even going against what your rational mind feels is best. Take action to create the change your heart is calling for in order to reestablish your internal sense of empowerment and joy.

Embarrassed/Humiliated: Derivative of Sadness and Anxiety

Ego Message: I don't like that others saw this side of me. I feel ashamed for my mistake, or for acting like a fool.

Empowered Self's Message: Embarrassment is calling you to honor your vulnerabilities. In other words, what embarrasses you is what you are called to embrace. Embracing this part of you strengthens you, inspiring you to ask for help, cultivate deeper intimacy, or add humor by not taking yourself so seriously. You needn't make an embarrassing situation define you in a negative way. Rather than judge this part of yourself as inadequate or weak, how can you give this part of yourself understanding and compassion? You are being called to deepen your self-love by knowing you are whole in each moment. Being whole, you accept the perfection and imperfection in all that you are, which enables you to see yourself with greater love, compassion, and humor!

Empty: Derivative of Sadness

Ego Message: I feel I have nothing to give or offer. There is an endless pit within me that cannot be filled.

Empowered Self's Message: You have been trying to fill an internal void by external means. Now is your time to address internal needs from within yourself rather than look to others for a fleeting sense of being okay. A state of nothingness is the perfect canvas on which to begin planting the seeds of your desires. See your old stories as weeds that will be pushed aside as your new dreams take root and are nourished.

Envy (See jealousy.)

Exposed (See vulnerable.)

Fearful: (See scared.)

Fed up: Derivative of Frustration and Anger

<u>Ego Message:</u> I am tired of how things are going. I can no longer tolerate this situation.

<u>Empowered Self's Message:</u> Your amped-up feelings allow you to see the truth of this situation and give you the courage to act. Your current reality isn't working and it is time to take a stand. Trust that when you act from love, it is for the overall good of everyone involved.

Foolish: Derivative of Sadness

<u>Ego Message:</u> What are others thinking of me? I feel dumb, naïve, and ridiculous.

<u>Empowered Self's Message:</u> You fear how others think of you in this moment because you suspect this may be the truth about who you are. You judge this part of yourself as weak or wrong, while your essence knows this part of you as your strength. The spiritual message in feeling foolish is to gain confidence in the truth of who you are. Your essence is guiding you to express yourself authentically and fully in each moment. With this greater sense of self-trust, you are able to continue to take risks in concert with your essence. This is when you feel free and full of joy!

Forsaken: Derivative of Sadness

<u>Ego Message:</u> I have been forgotten. My needs don't matter. I am not good enough to have my desires met.

<u>Empowered Self's Message:</u> When you base your value on others' actions/non-actions, YOU have forgotten your true

worth. This energy coming forward is a signal that you must remember your truth, which is that YOU ARE PURE LOVE! Regardless of what you have done or said, regardless of whether you have done wrong or been wronged, YOU ARE LOVE. You are being called RIGHT NOW to nourish your essence in deeply loving ways.

Grief-stricken: Derivative of Sadness

Ego Message: I am in a state of shock. My sense of normalcy, security, and comfort is gone. Life will never be happy for me again.

Empowered Self's Message: You are experiencing profound change and must mourn your loss fully. This is a time of transition that will ultimately reveal more of your inner light, power, strength, and compassion for life. Allow yourself to tread softly and feel fully as you find your way back to your center.

Heavy: Derivative of Sadness and Guilt

Ego Message: I feel weighed down, unable to move forward with life as I would like to.

Empowered Self's Message: Feeling heavy signals that you are carrying too many of your ego's demands and obligations. You must evaluate what is truly important to you, and why. Don't take "I can't" as an answer. Recognize the story or role attached to any demands that feel nonnegotiable, and recognize too that choices do exist. Your essence wants you to feel joy, freedom, and lightness, which is accessed by letting go of that which does not serve your highest good.

Helpless: Derivative of Frustration and Sadness

<u>Ego Message:</u> I have exhausted all my options. I don't have the support I need. I don't know what to do, or which way to turn to get the help I need. Nothing I am doing is leading me to the help I need.

<u>Empowered Self's Message</u>: You feel stuck because you are lost in a limited mindset. This mindset convinces you that you have tried just about everything to create the change you desire. Your rational mind is limiting you to the belief that doing x, y, or z will bring the outcome you desire. As always, another choice is possible. Usually this choice involves being bolder than you would like, as well as addressing the shame that keeps you from recognizing this choice as your best option. Ultimately, your helplessness is present to help you to recognize that you are powerful beyond your wildest imagination. But you can claim this power only when you choose the discomfort of facing your fears, instead of the familiar comfort of your victim story.

Hopeless: Derivative of Sadness and Frustration

<u>Ego message:</u> I have lost hope. I give up. There is no way out of this situation.

<u>Empowered Self's Message:</u> Hopelessness is what happens when you don't listen to the loving guidance of your frustration. It tells you that this area of your life cannot get better if you continue living the way you are living. Unconsciously, you are tied to an old mindset that cannot work for your highest good because it is based on ego messages and fears. Keep plodding along on the same path and your hopelessness will turn to depression. It is time to reclaim your essence

and truth, which holds the true light to your path. (Outside support is recommended.)

Impatient: Derivative of Frustration

<u>Ego Message:</u> I am tired of waiting. Why don't I have what my heart desires? What more can I do? What am I doing wrong?

<u>Empowered Self's Message:</u> What you are doing isn't working because your ego wants to push to make your desire a reality. When you push, you are coming from a place of tension and lack, and your energy contracts, making it more difficult for you to receive. Your essence is calling you to take a calm step back so that you may appreciate the abundance in what your current reality offers. In other words, see how you can still thrive and be happy in your current reality, even if you never receive your desire. That is how you are being called to live; otherwise, you are at least partially defining yourself based upon whether or not you achieve your dream. When you determine to live your best life with what you already have, you are lovingly and lightly holding your current reality. And in this nonresistance, you become a vessel, open to receive. Sink into the loving nurturance of your essence to remember the feminine way, which is to bring forward what makes you happy and fulfilled in your current reality.

Inadequate: Derivative of Sadness

<u>Ego Message:</u> I am not enough. I am lacking.

<u>Empowered Self's Message:</u> When you feel inadequate about your relationship, your career, your finances, or your kids, you are looking outside of yourself to find your value. Your value, however, is not to be found outside of yourself. Should

you seek your value outside of yourself, you GUARANTEE you will never be adequate enough according to the expectations and standards of your implacable ego. No, the path to joy and fulfillment is not found through the ego; it is found in your essence. Use the discomfort of feeling inadequate to sound the alarm whenever your ego tries to take you down yet another cul-de-sac. The loving energy of feeling inadequate is there for you to get clear on how perfect you and your current conditions actually are as the springboard to an increasingly fulfilled life.

Insecure: Derivative of Anxiety and Sadness

Ego Message: I see myself as "less than," compared to others.

Empowered Self's Message: The gift of insecurity is being able to take a look at who or what standards you are comparing yourself with, which reveals exactly what is triggering your sense of lack. Insecurity asks you to recognize the shame theme you are using to define yourself. For example, when you feel insecure about not being in a romantic relationship, you are defining yourself as unlovable; when you feel insecure about not making more money, you are defining yourself as not good or smart or clever enough. Your inner work is to recognize how your beliefs create your reality, and to be willing to choose a different belief that serves your highest good.

Insulted: Derivative of Anger

Ego Message: I feel disrespected and dishonored. My true self is not seen.

Empowered Self's Message: An insult has the power to

disturb you only when a part of you fears that the insult is appropriate. You of course don't want the insult to apply to you because you judge this insulted part of you as wrong or bad. Your essence wants you to recognize what you fear about yourself in order to reclaim this part of you. Remember, every aspect of you has a healthy expression. A latent gift exists within any part you feel ashamed of, a gift that will serve your purposes when you incorporate this aspect back into yourself.

Intimidated: Derivative of Anxiety and Sadness

Ego Message: I am afraid I won't measure up and/or don't know what I am doing. I feel incapable, less than other people, or afraid that I will fail.

Empowered Self's Message: Your essence is trying to show you that you are afraid of your internal power, as you feel more comfortable in playing small. Playing small allows you to feel safer than if you were to claim your full expression of self. Every true challenge carries an element of intimidation; otherwise, it wouldn't feel like a challenge. You are being called to expand. Let go of expectations and judgments. Stay in the present moment. Play, be vulnerable, and open yourself up to what the situation can teach you.

Irritated (See annoyed.)

Jealousy: Derivative of Sadness/Frustration/Anxiety

Ego Message: Someone else has what I want but have not been able to get. This makes me feel less than, inferior, or not good enough. I am lacking.

Empowered Self's Message: The spiritual energy of jealousy

calls you to change your perceptions and actions to reflect your equal worth to those who have already realized their desires. They are you, the only difference being that they have learned to cultivate their gifts rather than dismiss or diminish their significance. Jealousy enables you to see in another the energy and vision necessary to fulfill your desires. Jealousy is the mirror showing what's possible for you when you believe in yourself!

Limited: Derivative of Frustration/Anger/Sadness

Ego Message: I don't have all I need.

Empowered Self's Message: We all have limitations, whether with time or money or something else. The question is how you choose to work with them: from a state of expansion or one of contraction. Contraction occurs when you believe in the story behind your lack. Expansion occurs when you recognize the abundance within the limitations. From an expanded viewpoint, you open yourself up to the guidance coming from your inner wisdom. Open to receive, you recognize limitation as an illusion.

Longing: Derivative of Sadness and Frustration

Ego Message: What I desire feels out of reach or almost impossible to attain.

Empowered Self's Message: You ego is having you live in the future — in a wishful "someday",scenario. When you are in the future, you are not completely in the present moment. Being in the present moment is what allows you to claim your internal power. To support your expansion into a life that is truly fulfilling, trust that your current reality is perfect for you.

Lost: Derivative of Sadness

<u>Ego Message:</u> I don't know what I am doing with my life or who I really am.

<u>Empowered Self's Message:</u> When you feel lost, your essence is trying to tell you that you are not in alignment with your truth because your energy is too scattered. You are in your mind, or in the past and/or future. To realign with your true path means you must bring yourself back into your body (where you can listen to your heart) and to the present moment. Let go of judgment and act immediately upon your heart.

Manipulated: Derivative of Anger/Sadness

<u>Ego Message:</u> I've been unfairly taken advantage of.

<u>Empowered Self's Message:</u> To be manipulated means you have given your power away to another. You do this when you attach shame to your needs. Typical ways we do this is by feeling unworthy, not deserving or good enough to ask for what we need. You then end up compromising yourself in an attempt to get your needs met. You are being called to more deeply commit to your essence by being clear, forthright, and unapologetic about your needs.

Misunderstood: Derivative of Sadness and Anxiety

<u>Ego Message:</u> People don't "get" me. There is a disconnect between the meaning of what I say and the meaning that others interpret from what I share.

<u>Empowered Self's Message:</u> Your essence is calling you to a better understanding of your true self. You are judging

aspects of yourself as being wrong. Because you don't want these aspects to be seen, they often pop out in Freudian slips, or come out garbled when you unconsciously try to disguise what you're thinking. Your empowered self uses this feeling to remind you to be aware of those qualities you wouldn't want others to see in you. This is your guidance as to what you need to accept and incorporate. In this way, you encourage healthy expressions of all aspects of yourself, and are thus freer to be your true self!

Negative: Derivative of Sadness and Guilt

Ego Message: I am having a bad day. Nothing feels good or right in my life currently.

Empowered Self's Message: You energy has become tied up in a lie. This lie is the shame you carry about who you are, and you are now acting unconsciously from a place of shame. Being able to feel your negativity is a sign that you are ready and able to address your shame from love. You are being called to get clear on what you really want and need from your heart, and determine what beliefs about yourself will help you realize your deepest desires.

Nervous: Derivative of Anxiety

Ego Message: I feel on edge. I don't feel in complete control.

Empowered Self's Message: The energy of being nervous is to rev you up and awaken you from your normal state. Your mind wants to wrap you up in "what-if?" scenarios, which keep you away from your power. Your power lies in the present moment as you take action based on your inner guidance rather than fear. Let this enlivening energy inspire trust in your inner guidance. It will never fail you.

Obligated: Derivative of Guilt

Ego Message: I feel required to do what I don't want to do, or bound by a sense of duty.

Empowered Self's Message: When obligation feels heavy rather than light, it means that you are in performance mode. You are not in alignment with your truth because YOU are defining yourself too narrowly. You are being called to act from a place of compassion for yourself. See your main obligation as being true to your heart, without judgment. Your heart knows what is right for all involved.

Overwhelmed: Derivative of Anxiety and Guilt

Ego Message: There is so much that I need to do and not enough time, energy, or money to get it all done.

Empowered Self's Message: Feeling overwhelmed is a signal that you are off too far into the future. Take time to settle back into your body. Ask your essence what next step you should take. Your power is in taking one mindful step at a time.

Panicky: Derivative of Anxiety

Ego Message: I am feeling completely out of control. I can't think straight and don't know what to do.

Empowered Self's Message: Panic serves to alert you that you are living at the whim of the monkey-mind and are losing your true sense of self. Immediately ground yourself by taking cleansing breaths (long inhales through your nose, extended exhales out through your mouth) and by getting yourself close to nature (water, trees, plants, flowers, vegetables, etc.). This is a strong indicator that you must initiate action toward reclaiming your authentic self with complete commitment, dedication, and focus.

Powerless: Derivative of Anger

Ego Message: I can't do anything. I have no options or choice.

Empowered Self's Message: The ways you have tried to claim your power have unconsciously been tied to filling an ego need. Your essence is guiding you to connect to your true power. Often this involves letting go of ego notions about how you define your thoughts, behavior, or self. Remember, even prisoners have the power to determine what their circumstances mean to them and how they will react to them.

Pressure: Derivative of Anxiety

Ego Message: I can't keep up with the demands imposed by myself or others. I feel pushed to my limits.

Empowered Self's Message: Your fears have driven you to run your life by force rather than trust. Your ego has you believe that pushing yourself is the only way to meet demands. Because pushing is a tightening and constrictive energy, you aren't able to share your best self. Instantly relieve pressure by listening to your heart and enter into a state of allowing. Allowing acknowledges the space in which you are receptive to attracting and receiving, rather than forcing things to happen according to your ego/others' demands. This inner rebalancing opens you to your next steps as well as new opportunities your limited mind would never have considered.

Rage: Amped-up Anger (that needs immediate attention)

Read the chapter on anger.

Ego Message: I feel out of my mind. I need to lash out right now.

Empowered Self's Message: You are being called to act from a new state of power you have yet to claim. Claim your truth from love and walk away from what you believe is enraging you. The violation you wish to correct comes from within yourself. When you honor your boundaries with love, honor and passion for your highest good, others will instinctively know not to cross you.

Regret: Derivative of Guilt and Sadness

Ego Message: I look back upon my actions and wish I had done things differently. I made a bad choice. I fear there is nothing I can do to remedy the situation.

Empowered Self's Message: Your ego is tying you to the past, where you remain powerless. Your power is in the present. First, reclaim your worth through forgiveness of self. Although you may or may not be able to "fix" the situation, love will bring forth healing and transformational insight. Then take responsibility for your part and move toward addressing the situation from the guidance of your heart. Apply what you learned to your life. Forgive yourself, but don't forget what you have learned.

Rejected: Derivative of Sadness/Anger

Ego Message: I am not accepted. I feel judged that I somehow don't measure up or that I am not enough.

Empowered Self's Message: The rejection you experienced

holds a mirror to your internal fears about yourself, now brought into your awareness. Whatever the reason you feel rejected is exactly what you need to more fully honor about yourself. As you integrate this part of yourself back into your identity, you gain greater certainty about who you truly are and the gifts you have to offer.

Remorse: Derivative of Guilt and Sadness

Ego Message: I feel terrible about myself and past actions. I cannot forgive myself.

Empowered Self's Message: The spiritual energy of remorse helps you to see your actions through the eyes of compassion. Compassion encourages you to review the incident you feel remorseful about and witness what is triggering your fear. Identifying the fear, you learn from the situation and grow so you can live more fully aligned with your highest version of you.

Resentful: Derivative of Anger

Ego Message: Someone or something has wronged me. I feel dishonored.

Empowered Self's Message: Your ego makes you believe that your anger is directed at another or a situation. Resentment is present to support you in the healing of the anger you have toward yourself. The real source of your resentment is the sense of powerlessness you feel. Your essence would have you reclaim your power by learning what made you unconsciously give it away.

Restless – See Anxiety.

Restricted – See Limited.

Run down: Derivative of Sadness and Frustration

<u>Ego Message:</u> I am worn out and depleted.

<u>Empowered Self's Message:</u> Being run down means that your ego is running you. You are barely aware of your essence, which is why you have nothing left to give. Make self-nourishment a priority by giving yourself time to address your needs and desires. While taking time for your essence through nurturance and play may feel counterintuitive, refueling your inner self leads to being more efficient and effective in life.

Scared: Derivative of Anxiety

Read the chapter on fear.

<u>Ego Message:</u> I am afraid. I do not feel completely safe.

<u>Empowered Self's Message:</u> Fear coming from your ego aims to keep you safe at all costs, including the cost of losing your authentic sense of self. Fear coming from love is present to awaken an expanded version of self. Its purpose is to help you move beyond your comfort zone and experience more of your divinity. You are being called to live your life based on truth rather than ego deceptions, making choices that best serve your highest version of you. Being scared from an empowered vantage point means get ready — now is your time to take a leap!

Self-Conscious: Derivative of Anxiety

<u>Ego Message:</u> I feel as if everyone is looking at me or judging me. I feel uncomfortable with myself.

<u>Empowered Self's Message:</u> The judgment or unwanted attention you feel coming from others is a projection of the exaggerated attention you are giving to aspects of yourself that you most harshly judge. Self-consciousness is your empowered self's way of bringing to awareness that which you need to accept within yourself. Rather than feel shame at these expressions of self, you are being guided to see their gifts, and integrate them into the totality of who you really are. You may also feel self-conscious when you shine! Rather than overemphasize those aspects of yourself that you feel give you value, recognize them as only facets of the whole gift of who you are.

Self-Doubt - See Doubtful.

Shame – See Ashamed.

Shocked: Derivative of Sadness

<u>Ego Message</u>: I am in disbelief. How could this have happened?

<u>Empowered Self's Message:</u> Something took you by such surprise that it knocked you off your feet and uprooted your sense of being grounded. Your empowered self sees this as a good time to awaken to more of your truth and more of your strength. Whatever was so shocking to you tells you about where you are ready to grow and evolve. You are being called to awaken and claim more of yourself because you have outgrown an old belief system that kept you in denial. Start with the part that is hardest for you to accept, and look to reconcile that part from the heart of love. Then ask: What is love asking me to do?

Sorry for Myself: Derivative of Sadness

<u>Ego Message</u>: I have reason to feel sad. I have been unjustly hurt. I am a victim who has suffered pain.

<u>Empowered Self's Message</u>: Your essence is guiding you to expand upon your version of self. Mourn what has hurt you but don't define yourself based on that particular outcome. Instead, ask what you are meant to learn from the experience. Ask yourself: In what ways am I seeing myself as being limited? What would an expanded view of myself look like? Begin taking steps immediately toward an expanded view of self.

Tension: Derivative of Anxiety

<u>Ego Message</u>: I feel like I am walking on eggshells, or that I need to be on the defense.

<u>Empowered Self's Message</u>: Something is being avoided that needs to be addressed. Regardless of whether the other person involved is acting out of ego, you can act out of love. Take yourself out of the dramatic stories. Share your inner truth along with facts. Pray for guidance that keeps you aligned with love, for yourself and whomever else is involved.

Trapped: Derivative of Frustration

<u>Ego Message</u>: I feel as if there is no way out. I feel closed in and that I have nowhere to turn to get myself out of this situation.

<u>Empowered Self's Message</u>: Your essence wants you to recognize that you are trapped because the way you are living is not true to yourself. You are closing yourself off from the

support and assistance of your inner wisdom because following your inner guidance involves risk. You are being called to let go of the short-term results in order to make room for the long-term outcome your heart desires. You will continue to feel this tightness until you are radically willing to break free. You are being supported to make this leap.

Unsupported: Derivative of Sadness and/or Frustration

<u>Ego Message:</u> I have too much resting on my shoulders. I feel weighed down by responsibilities.

<u>Empowered Self's Message:</u> You are tied up in an illusion of control and a sense that you must do it all in order that your needs be met. Your ego attaches to this illusion of control to meet your needs regarding self-worth. Your essence is calling you to move from the role of doing to the truth of being. **Being is what allows you to lead,** because in being, you hold a vision. You thus recognize your power more clearly and allow the rest to be received. Now others are given space to come forward as you hold the vision clearly and unapologetically through love. In doing so, you empower others to serve at their highest level. As you lead from the heart, you open yourself up to receive.

Unwanted – See Rejected.

Unworthy: Derivative of Sadness and Guilt

<u>Ego Message:</u> I am not a good enough person to deserve fulfillment of my heart's desires.

<u>Empowered Self's Message:</u> Who decides whether you are or are not worthy? Only when you come from fear are you not enough. When you are connected to love, love sees your

worth in every single aspect of you. So who is doing the judging? Rather than look to the external to affirm your worth, follow the lead of your essence — from love to love. Your heart is asking: "In what ways do I allow love to flow through me?" Then you will experience your true worth.

Used: Derivative of Anger and Sadness

Ego Message: I have been taken advantage of and I don't like it!

Empowered Self's Message: Your ego wants to say, "How could he/she/they do that to me?" But what your essence would have you ask is, "How could I allow myself to be treated that way?" When you make decisions based on fear, you compromise yourself. You are being called to recommit to living in alignment with your essence by living more fully in integrity. You are worth more. Now claim it.

Useless: Derivative of Frustration and Sadness

Ego Message: I have no purpose. I have nothing to offer that anyone wants.

Empowered Self's Message: Right now your essence is telling you that your energy is almost completely consumed by your ego's message of not being good enough. Because of your belief in not being good enough, you look outside of yourself to validate your worth. What your essence wants you to recognize is that you feel useless because you are unconsciously refusing to use your inner guidance to direct your next steps. In other words, YOU are refusing to use your gifts when you ignore your inner guidance. Your inner guidance is attempting to support you in creating a fulfilling life, yet it can't when judged by your ego as unimportant or irrelevant. Begin listening to the whispers within, and take action regardless of what your ego thinks. Express your energy without expectation of what you will get in return. The value in all that you do is ultimately measured by what brings you joy. "Follow your bliss," as mythologist Joseph Campbell recommended, by acting on your inner guidance. Doing so will free you to be of service in the world as you are meant to be.

Violated: Derivative of Anger and Sadness

Ego Message: Something happened to me that should not have.

Empowered Self's Message:

When a violation occurs, it is trying to take you away from the truth of who you are. A part of you has been hurt, but rather than allow the ego to define you based on that incident, give voice to the part of you that has been hurt. This is how you regain strength and certainty in the loving truth of who you truly are. Use this strength to guide you in fully expressing your power through love. The more violated you feel, the more you will be guided to seek support in healing from this violation you experienced.

Vulnerable: Derivative of Anxiety and Sadness

Ego Message: I feel too exposed. I feel weak and am afraid I'll be hurt.

Empowered Self's Message: Being overly exposed makes you feel unsafe. A part of your armor was pierced or removed (at least temporarily) and yes, that feels scary to your ego when it is judging that part of you as weak or wrong. Your empowered self would have you recognize vulnerability not as a frightened whimper but rather a clear call for you to bring acceptance to this aspect of you so disdained by your ego. It is your opportunity for greater self-acceptance in recognizing and accepting that something feels sensitive to the touch. Through self-acceptance — fully owning who you are — you recognize how you can still be in your truth AND in your power. Your vulnerability actually increases your power because you are accepting yet another aspect of the real you. And the more you accept all aspects of yourself, the more you are able to relish your uniqueness and experience joy! If you feel vulnerable too often, it means you are exposing too much too fast. You are putting the responsibility of accepting you onto someone else and not yourself. Your own self-acceptance is what opens the way to true intimacy with others.

Worried: Derivative of Anxiety

Ego Message: Perhaps I can control a matter by over-thinking and analyzing, taking precautions, and always being on guard.

Empowered Self's Message: Worry is an illusion of control. This false illusion keeps you in the future or in the past. When you are in the future or past, you are removed from your inner guidance and the present, which is where your true power lies. Your essence uses worry as a signal that you are running on your rational mind and need to go back to your heart. Your heart may not give you the favored result that your ego craves in order to feel safe. What your heart will give you is your next step. Take that step into greater self-trust. Remember: When you worry, you are in the illusion of control. Let it go, as worry is the thief of your joy!

FEMININE EMOTIONAL MASTERY

AS YOU BEGIN THIS LAST CHAPTER, I WOULD LIKE YOU TO first welcome into your awareness all that has changed for you. Take a deep breath and really take in how a part of you knows without a doubt there is LOVE in all that you F.E.E.L. **Be proud of yourself** for making this integral internal shift.

Your awareness of love in everything you feel brings an awareness of choice: to bring your emotions close to you. You now recognize how your emotions are present to serve you. As you continue to integrate your feelings back into you, you are also beginning to taste and savor the love that exists in every emotion you experience.

Your ego will continue to try to cajole you back into the Emotional Stone Age. Yet, the ego's arguments won't hold as much appeal as they once did. You can now see how, when the benign intent of emotions was not understood, your ego gave meaning to your "negative" feelings, leaving your understanding one-sided. From this limited viewpoint, you formed beliefs, patterns, and actions which did not serve you but demanded expression.

Now you are able to recognize how the Emotional Stone Age unintentionally keeps us all smaller and struggling by unconsciously inculcating self-hatred via our negative feelings. Resistance to these negative feelings serves only to strengthen the fear and judgment of those "faults" that we seem to be fighting against. Sitting with our feelings has felt tedious when all we could hear was the ego barking negative messages. Peeking out from under the weight of our negative emotions, the light was hard to discern.

Because you now have access to deeper insight through F.E.E.L., you can make more informed and wise choices that serve your highest good. You understand the greater meaning behind your ego and fears working together to protect you until you are ready to live on purpose and in full expression. As you can more clearly recognize your ego and fears at play, the easier it has become for you to listen and act upon the loving guidance of your negative feelings.

At the same time, the true meaning of the "Big Five" is in the process of settling deep within you. Even if you still have moments when you get triggered by your ego's trickeries and critical messages (and you will), you won't stay there long. You know too much now. You simply cannot go back to living and reacting as you once did. It would feel false and wrong. You now see the loving meaning and purpose in all that you feel.

Should you temporarily "forget" (in other words, become overwhelmed by) a specific negative feeling, you can quickly refer to the derivative emotions guide to get yourself back on track. This allows for a rapid reset to living from your heart, rather than from egoic fear. As soon as you take the prescribed love-based action tied to the specific negative feeling you experienced, you know a positive shift will occur. In this life-affirming action, not only do your negative feelings dissipate more readily, but your life is transformed bit by bit into a much fuller expression of you!

You now see that the purpose of your negative feelings is twofold:

To wake you up when you are unconsciously living from fear rather than love, AND

To show you how to get "back to the garden" of your love state!

Knowing the purpose of your negative emotions changes everything. You no longer have to worry about going off the deep end in reactivity. Now that you recognize the loving guidance available to you, you can respond from your highest self. You know what your heart is asking you to do next, and you have the energy of your negative feeling to propel you forward to take action.

Just as exciting, your emotional energy is no longer wasted! By understanding the loving messages back of your negative feelings, what was once an energetic leak now becomes energetic fuel! F.E.E.L. is simply more energy efficient, allowing you to respond to your desires with greater wisdom and ease.

THE LAW OF ALLOWING: UTILIZING EMOTIONAL ENERGY TO CO-CREATE FROM YOUR HEART

A tremendous gift of learning how to F.E.E.L. is being able to experience your negative feelings with much greater ease. As you <u>allow</u> the gift of each feeling to work through you, you confidently step into the universal flow. Rather than trying to swim upstream every time you experience a negative feeling, *allowing* brings you back to a flow state. Once in the flow, you are more intuitive, receptive, and expansive. Most of all, you are not in fear because allowing means complete trust in this higher wisdom coming through your feelings to guide you.

Also in sync with universal principles, being able to allow your negative feelings to come through you also facilitates greater alignment with your intentions. Here's why. Most of you know about the Law of Attraction. Some of you may fully understand this fundamental law, yet wonder how you can make it more noticeable in your life. Others of you may question the Law of Attraction's validity. Regardless of your stance, what is clear is that not recognizing the loving essence in our negative feelings has impacted our ability to apply all of the Law of Attraction's principles.

Let me explain. The act of manifesting – realizing what you want to experience, which you've determined is for the highest good of all — actually consists of three laws. The most well-known law and also the most powerful is the Law of Attraction. The Law of Attraction states that "That which is like unto itself, is drawn." The second component is the Law of Deliberate Creation, which informs us that "That which we give thought to, we begin to attract into our experience." Whatever we think about, with ardent emotion, we attract more quickly. The third is the Art of Allowing, which states: "I am that which I am. While I am that which I am, I allow others to be that which they are." Further, by deliberately choosing thoughts that feel good, we achieve vibrational alignment with our Source of Well-Being.

When these three dynamics are understood and honored, you are working in harmony with yourself and the Universal Energy available to you. In the emotional Stone Age, the Law of Attraction cannot be used to its fullest because you find yourself in a Catch-22 where you seem damned if you do and damned if you don't. You create therefore, largely by default.

Some people, still emotional Stone Agers, misunderstand the Law of Attraction. Wishing to always be "positive," and thus attract positive things, they view negative feelings as being negative. What this means to Law of Attraction enthusiasts is that feeling negative feelings is to be avoided simply because like attracts like. Understood only from the perspective of the ego, negative feelings become the enemy. You don't want what your negative feelings attract to you when they are defined by the ego!

When emotions are defined through the limits of the ego, the result is that the first part of the Art of Allowing is ignored, while the second half – dealing with the responses of other people — becomes the focus. The art is in accepting not only ourselves, but others as they are, without judgment. The fundamental problem is that you haven't been able to fully accept yourself because you haven't learned to accept your negative feelings.

The Art of Allowing rests on the truth that *I am that which I am*. This means that you accept and love yourself just as much when you are mad or sad as when you are calm or joyful. In the emotional Stone Age, when anger is seen as poisonous or destructive, you fear accepting a reality such as "I am angry." Such resistance leaves you trying to pretend you feel differently, tensely striving to free yourself from how you authentically feel. In other words, there is no room for acceptance of the negative.

Emotional awareness brings acceptance of ourselves. You can finally be at peace with who you truly are in any given moment. You are always radiating love, even when experiencing a negative feeling. From the new model of emotional awareness, you truly become aligned with Universal Thought and Intention. No longer does there need to be internal conflict and struggle when negative feelings pop up, because now you have all your energy working for you. With all your emotional energy working for you, your emotions become the fuel to your intentions, supporting you to co-create your desires with the Universal Energy available to you!

YOUR NEXT STEP - CONSCIOUS EMOTIONAL MASTERY

Living in an emotionally conscious way means that fear becomes optional once you understand your feelings from love. Your negative feelings become invaluable warnings whenever you are operating from fear. Your next step is for this loving guidance to become second nature to you. In other words, you are ready for emotional mastery.

Conscious emotional mastery is feminine mastery, which means the focus is on power *with* rather than power *over* your feelings. Through this feminine viewpoint, emotions are artistic tools that shape your own special beauty. You now recognize how emotions are able to weave through you, actually strengthening your sense of self. By acknowledging your feelings from love, you honor more of yourself as love. Pure love is what you essentially are, and what you have come here to remember.

Key to this next step is not minding when your ego freaks out at the word "mastery!" Mastery is simply practice. Conscious emotional mastery means you are willing to practice connecting to the loving message each and every time you experience a negative feeling. Of course, you will continue to hear the ego's crazy fantasies and lies whenever you experience a negative feeling. The point is that the ego version of yourself becomes quieter while the loving guidance becomes more audible and accessible.

To attain to a level of emotional mastery, you are going to have to follow your loving guidance, even when doing so scares the living daylights out of you! You need at least one time when following the guidance of your inner wisdom is in complete opposition to your rational mind. For most of us, this means being willing to let go.

Remember, your inner wisdom is willing to sacrifice short-term discomfort in order to have your needs met over the long term. Letting go of temporary ease and satisfaction may feel as if you are walking away from your dream. The truth of the matter is that hanging on to something that isn't completely fulfilling is holding on to fear. You are being called to act in trust and faith in the highest version of you.

The greater purpose of your feelings is to deepen your relationship with yourself, your inner guidance, and the ocean of wisdom behind it. As your relationship with your true self deepens, your life's path becomes clear, challenges don't knock you off course as much, and you more easily remain in a flow state of living. Living in flow means being connected to your heart, regardless of life's circumstances.

Now, with your negative feelings on your side, all you need do is stay in greater connection with your heart. Resting in the heart, you will be able to more clearly hear its whispers guiding you to act from love rather than fear. Your next step is to get used to being uncomfortable with what your inner guidance is telling you to do — and act on it.

We are often told to get our lives together so that we may become of greater service. But when ego is the driving force, true service is often impossible. How can we serve when our health is out of whack due to unhealthy eating, or when our work leaves us depleted, or our relationships weigh heavily on us? The empathy, joy, and creative solutions we would offer our fellows are simply unavailable, obscured by self-concern.

This isn't about perfection. It's about letting your emotions guide you to clear up the distractions that take you away from your true calling. As you get these integral aspects of your life together, you are then able to serve at your highest level and share your gifts with the world.

All it takes is trusting in yourself just one time, and not backing down from your choice. I guarantee you will see great rewards from following your heart. Immediate results may sometimes not be exactly what you hoped for, yet in the long term, you draw ever closer to the expression of your heart's desire. Then use that experience to strengthen and inspire you to take the next leap. Through these small leaps of faith, you build strength to take bigger and bigger leaps, guiding you to realize your fullest expression of you! This is the path to conscious emotional mastery, the feminine way to use your emotions that allows you to more consistently SHINE!

LIGHTING THE PATH AS AN EMOTIONAL LUMINARY

The illusion of darkness that was once experienced in your negative feelings is currently fading. You made your way through the tunnel of darkness to recognize that the light was there all along, as it always is and has been. A power that had lain latent in the darkness of your negative feelings is now illuminated by the love within your heart. In reclaiming this power, a "new you" is born: one that is filled with love, energy, strength, and courage to move forward on your path.

By reading this book, you have unknowingly answered a calling to become an Ambassador of **un**-ending, limit-**less** <u>self-love</u>. You become an exemplar of the seemingly impossible: you find love where it was once lost on each of us. As easily as you breathe, you also radiate love. Now, **even when you feel sadness, anger, frustration, or anxiety, you still know how extremely loved and cared for you are.** What people experience is that despite how you feel, you radiate love.

As love radiates from you, you naturally become a magnet to others. They too want the love within themselves to be fully awakened and expressed. Ultimately, we don't just want this for ourselves; deep down, all people yearn to share their love with others.

I must be perfectly clear with you. Learning how to F.E.E.L. isn't just about you. You know the world is changing at record speed, and many, many people are experiencing challenges they never had to face previously. The more things change, the more emotions get stirred up. People are suffering emotionally, and desperately looking for another way. The way they are looking for calls for deeper self-love.

The level of self-love that is available makes no sense to the rational mind. Within the confines of our minds, it is inconceivable that love could exist in something that we consider as abhorrent as our negative emotions. You will be sharing how love and inner wisdom prevail over fear and intelligence alone.

In essence, what you are doing is demonstrating a way that encourages everyone to thrive, internally and externally, as we enter this new world. You love yourself with reckless abandon, in joy that's contagious. As you do, you find your life unfolding in unexpected ways that nourish and fulfill you wholly and completely. When others witness this within you, they know it is possible for themselves as well. This is when, unwittingly, you have become an Emotional Luminary, one who is a guiding light to those who remain in the darkness of the Emotional Stone Age.

Each of us is being called to reclaim what was once misunderstood, dishonored, and considered shameful within ourselves. As you reclaim your negative feelings, you feel more whole and connected. When you become more whole and connected, those around you become more whole and connected ...IF you are willing to show them that another way exists.

Ultimately, the way for people to feel whole and connected will be found within each and every one of us. Through this reclamation of self through love, we will gain the energy, insight, and focus to share our hearts. And the more deeply we can give of ourselves in this sea of love, the more the world is able to transform.

The only question remaining is: Are you willing to taste and share this depth of love? It is limitless, and available for you to share day by day, moment by moment, and emotion by emotion. In doing so, you teach yourself and others that each negative feeling is there to wake you up and serve as a springboard to bold, energetic leaps. And it is in plunging into who you really are that you may serve at your highest level as your fullest expression of you!

Shine on, Emotional Luminary! SHINE ON!

APPENDIX A

INNER DIALOGUE MEDITATION

THE FOLLOWING IS AN INNER DIALOGUE MEDITATION, WHICH supports you to connect and listen to the voice of your Inner Wisdom. It is important not to use this process to try to get rid of your negative feelings. This meditation allows you to bring all of your feelings closer to you through love rather than fear by reconnecting to the all-knowing place within you.

Let's Begin....

___

Take a few cleansing breathes. Imagine with each breath you are sinking deeper within your body.

Image a place deep within you, about 2-3 inches below your navel, as your sacred space. This sacred space is your home where you are always understood & always loved. There is no judgment about you here. You are totally free to be you and be honored, loved and accepted for who you are in this exact moment. This is where you are totally nurtured and take-care of because there is nothing you have to be or do.

Begin to imagine the scenery around you within your sacred space. Maybe you are outside in nature or within an inside setting. See if you can pick up on any images, colors or feelings you get being in your sacred space.

Feel yourself feeling more comfortable in your home. This is a place where you are welcome to open yourself to receive. Feel your heart expanding and opening even more to receive your Inner Wisdom. In this sacred space, you feel deep trust toward yourself and you know you are immensely loved. This space is where your dreams and the infinite possibilities of your true self is safe.

Now ask yourself, what does my Inner Wisdom want me to know about the current situation which has brought about my negative feelings? What am I meant to understand through these specific feelings?

Trust in whatever comes to you. You may receive an image, a word, a color, a smell. Just allow whatever wants to come through to you to be shared with you and give thanks for it all.

Ask if there is any other clarity your inner wisdom would like to reveal.

Now take whatever was revealed to you and imagine it as a gift that now rests in the palms of your hands. Take this gift that you hold in your palms and press it lovingly to your heart, where it's true significance is sealed. Know within your heart that the wisdom of these gifts are always available to you and will keep coming forward to you throughout the day.

Again, thank your inner wisdom for this gift and the blessings it contains. Give thanks for the connection you have with your Inner Wisdom, no matter how faint it may feel at this moment.

If you like, you may tell your Inner Wisdom you'll soon be back to visit. You may also give your okay for your negative feelings to be used as an invitation for you to come back to your inner home.

You are now departing from this home with a knowingness that this sacred space is always available to you because it was created uniquely for you. You may come back to it as often as you would like.

Slowly begin to travel back up through your body, up through your core to your heart center and now back into your current physical surroundings.

Immediately take 5 to 20 minutes to journal about what you received.

Allow whatever comes though your pen to be written without editing. You may also want to draw an image of what thoughts or feelings came through during the meditation. Even if there was nothing, let's say for instance a sense of emptiness- write or indicate what that means or felt like coming from your inner wisdom (ie. what's the benefit of that state?). The point is there is no such thing as receiving anything "wrong."

APPENDIX B

EVERYONE EXPERIENCES DIFFERENT VOICES GOING ON IN their heads. Typically, these voices can be narrowed down to two types of voices.

1. Your ego voice: This voice conveys messages that are self-destructive and is often referred to as: the critic, the judgmental voice, the hard on you voice, the voice that puts you down, the voice that tells you that you better keep doing more and more even though you are exhausted.

2. Your Essence Voice: This voice provides you with loving guidance. This is the voice that encourages you, the voice that loves you unconditionally, the voice that supports you to see your truth, the voice that empowers you. You may also call this voice your Inner Wisdom, your Empowered Self or whatever name fits for you.

By the time most people reach adolescents, they are used to hearing the voice of their ego far more than hearing the voice of their Essence. In order to hear the loving messages coming from your Essence, you have to consciously decide to build your relationship with your Essence.

To build your relationship with your Essence, you need to

take time to step back and really listen to what is going on within you rather than continue to fall back on auto-responses created by the unconscious fears of your ego.

Inner Dialoguing is simply a way for you to have a conversation with the parts of yourself that run in opposition of one another: your ego and your Essence. Inner Dialoging is about creating a back and forth conversation between your ego and Essence. You start by allowing your ego to go first. Allow it to come clean with what is really bothering you and all the pain associated with it.

Once the ego feels heard, allow your essence to share how love would respond to this situation your ego has presented. You can imagine yourself having a conversation with your Inner Wise Self, or even with the Divinity you celebrate. Your job is to simply write whatever comes through to you.

(If during your Essence's turn you feel like you have drawn a blank, give yourself the green light to express what is coming up for you. Let your concerns be expressed, whether you worry you lack connection to your Inner Wisdom or whatever else is troubling you. Then ask your Inner Wise Self, if these concerns are true and see what type of response you get. Then discern does the response sound like ego or Essence? If your ego is still taking the lead, share your feelings about this.)

Next allow your ego to respond to your inner wisdom. Often your ego will share its doubts and fears. Permit them to be shared openly. Again, allow your Essence to respond.

Keep the dialogue flowing until you feel clear as to how you are being guided to respond to the situation from love. All you are looking for is your next step and to take this step in confidence.

Some worry that the process will go on forever, as the ego tends to be such a brute. The ego will stop, however, because it will naturally run out of excuses. The same stories that try to deflate you or make you powerless keep appearing. By being on the look-out for such themes, you will soon find yourself bored by what the ego is telling you. You become less reactive to your ego's stories because you begin to recognize how often your ego has used these lies to take you away from your joy. This is when you start to realize that whatever sense of safety the ego is trying to persuade you toward is not worth the hefty price of losing your true self.

Keep the focus on <u>how</u> you are to move forward and <u>what</u> you are being called to do next from the standpoint of love. Questions that ask why fuel the ego's ability to make you feel powerless. Finish when you experience a clear step you can commit to taking action to in the near, if not immediate, future.

Give thanks to your Essence for the guidance you received.

Inner Dialoguing can look like the following -

Ego:

Essence:

Ego:

Essence:

Ego:

Essence:

And so on, until you feel complete.

You can also divide a sheet a paper in half with ego on one half of the page and Essence on the other.

Be prepared for your ego to say a lot more because the ego likes to whine and carry on. Your essence will be shorter, clearer and more succinct.

By trusting your inner wisdom, you strengthen your connection to your Essence and lessen the hold your ego has on you.

GIVING BACK

MY PERSONAL AND PROFESSIONAL WORK IS ABOUT LEARNING to access and celebrate our innate potential. I believe the more we can access our true potential, the more joyful and fulfilled we feel.

Kandu Industries has made accessing the potential for people with disabilities a possibility, where fifty years ago there was little to no opportunity available.

Kandu's mission is to create, promote and provide diverse opportunities within the community that offer persons with disabilities or disadvantages the opportunity to pursue greater independence and meet their full potential.

When I witness people addressing personal challenges and thriving, I am inspired. Kandu has been an inspiration for me and because of that a portion of the proceeds from each book are given to this powerful organization.

For more information on Kandu go to http://www.kandu-industries.com/

ACKNOWLEDGMENTS

THIS BOOK IS MADE POSSIBLE BY THE GUIDANCE, CARE AND support of so many amazing people I have been blessed to cross paths with along this journey.

My thanks to Jo-Ann Langseth for understanding the intricacies of this work, and providing insightful and meticulous editing. Thank you to Brion Sausser for creating a book cover design that went above and beyond what I imagined.

Many thanks to all those who handled the "behind the scenes" work. Your dedicated presence has allowed me to remain balanced. I especially want to thank Tanja for handling all the technical components and making my ideas come to life online.

The list of mentors and teachers, whom I have been fortunate to cross paths with throughout the years, could be a whole book in and of itself. I give thanks to all of you who have shared yourself and your lessons in order that I could take my work to greater depth and understanding.

Thank you to my dear friends, Donna Gilman and Suzanne Monroe, for listening to all my ideas, believing in my vision, and constantly cheering me on to get my work out into the world. I am so grateful for your attentive ears and huge, open hearts. You are my soul sisters, thank you for bringing so much loving, feminine energy into my life!

Thank you Mom and Dad for your support and love. Thank you, Mom, for always taking the time to comment on my posts and being my biggest Facebook fan. To my in-laws, Gar and Aud, thank you for always wanting to spread the word about my work and rooting for me.

My amazing children Avery, Jonah and Eli: Thank you, you are each an inspiration! I am so grateful for your reminders of the importance of play, and especially for all the hugs and kisses along the way.

To the most amazing husband in the world: I love you, Steve. Thank you isn't enough for all the ways in which you have shown your support in me, invested in me and, most importantly, believed in me. I am so blessed to have you and your incredible love by my side on this adventure!

My greatest thanks is to God. Thank you for teaching me how you speak to us all through our emotions and helping someone as sensitive as myself to find solace in my negative feelings. Thank you for your trust, your gentleness, and the depth of your love.

ABOUT THE AUTHOR

MICHELLE BERSELL, M.A., M.ED., IS KNOWN AS A VISIONARY leader in emotional consciousness who challenges common thought and understanding regarding emotional well-being. Combining her training as a psychotherapist along with her spiritual insight, Michelle continues to lead thousands to a new level of accessing and celebrating their potential through her seminars, retreats, speaking engagements, products, and individual and group programs.

Besides media attention in *Women's World* magazine, and *Parents* magazine, Michelle is featured in the upcoming film documentary *The Secret 2 LUCK*. Michelle's latest book *F.E.E.L.: Turn Your Negative Feelings Into Your Greatest Allies* was chosen as a featured gift of the 2012 Emmy Awards. She has also received national recognition as one of the "50 Great Authors You Should be Reading" for her first book *Emotional Abundance: Become Empowered.*

Michelle currently lives in Milwaukee, Wisconsin with her loving husband, daughter and twin sons.

Find out more about Michelle at:
www.MichelleBersell.com